TOC H

To:-
Michael
with all my love
on your 50th birthday
Hazel.
xxx 1981

Called Up

CD4
5514
RN

Called Up

A National Service Scrapbook

George Forty

LONDON
IAN ALLAN LTD

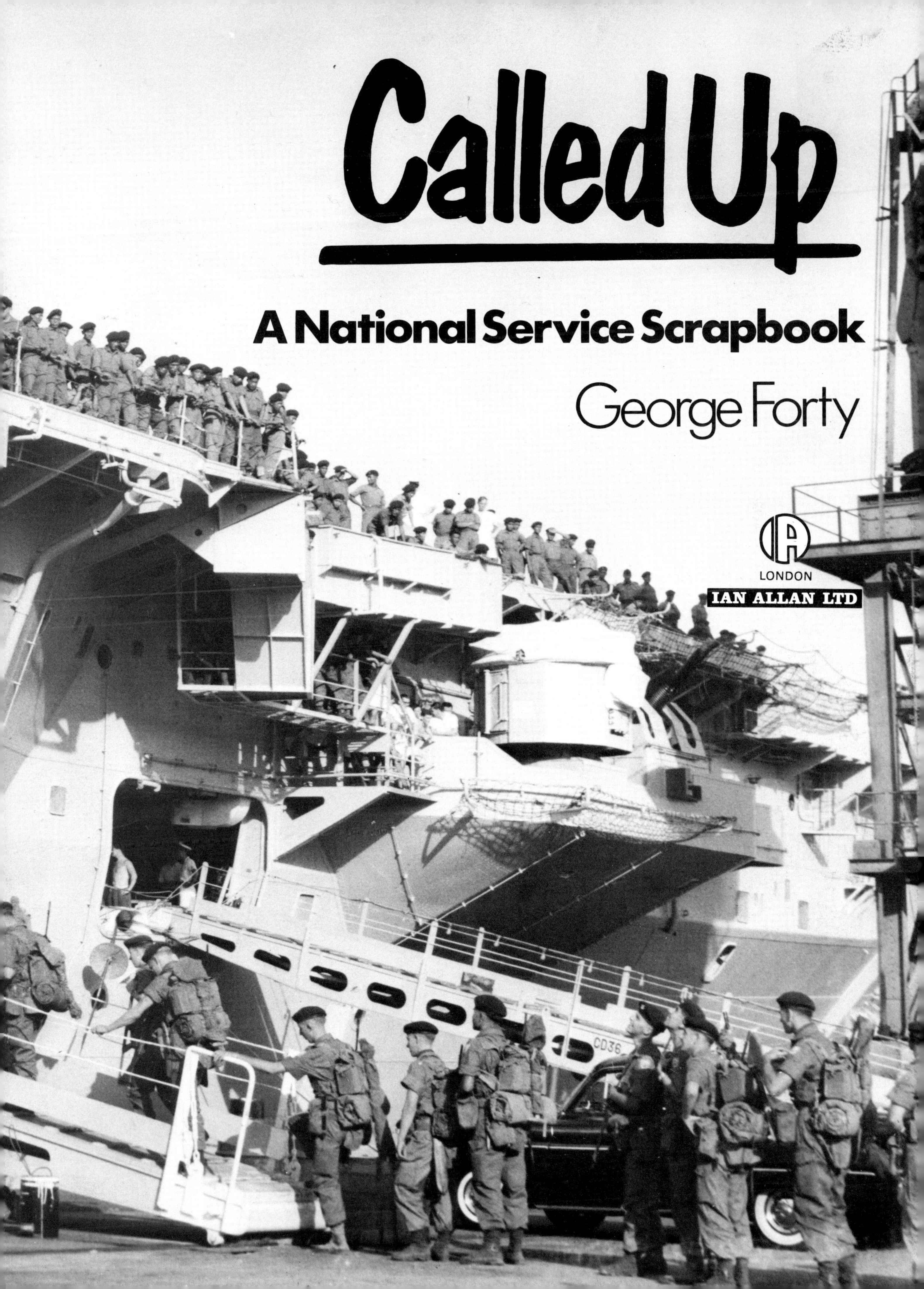

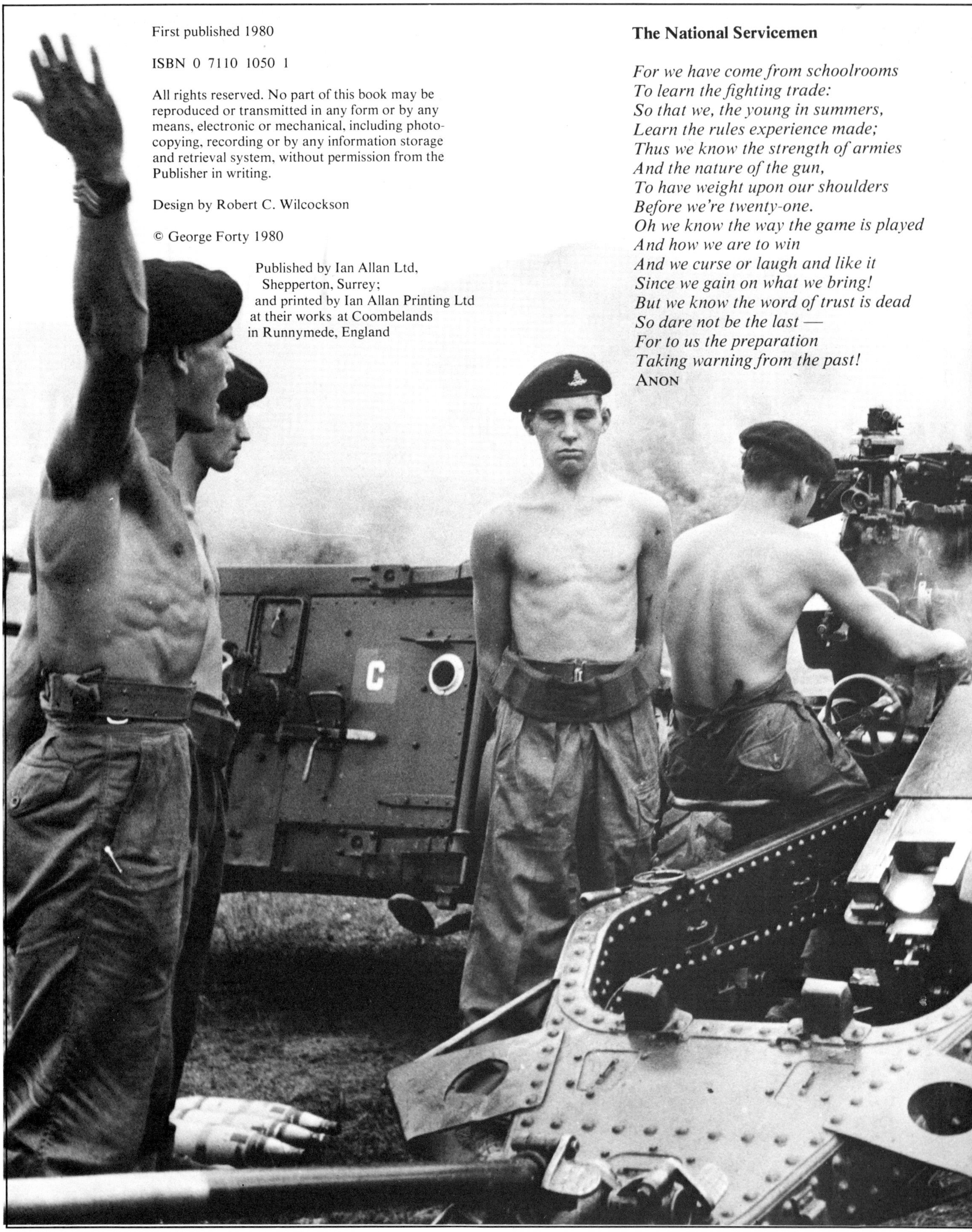

First published 1980

ISBN 0 7110 1050 1

Design by Robert C. Wilcockson

Published by Ian Allan Ltd,
Shepperton, Surrey;
and printed by Ian Allan Printing Ltd
at their works at Coombelands
in Runnymede, England

The National Servicemen

For we have come from schoolrooms
To learn the fighting trade:
So that we, the young in summers,
Learn the rules experience made;
Thus we know the strength of armies
And the nature of the gun,
To have weight upon our shoulders
Before we're twenty-one.
Oh we know the way the game is played
And how we are to win
And we curse or laugh and like it
Since we gain on what we bring!
But we know the word of trust is dead
So dare not be the last —
For to us the preparation
Taking warning from the past!
ANON

Contents

Introduction and Acknowledgements

If one discounts the Roman Army, which was based on conscript levies, then the history of National Service in Britain goes back to feudal times. There were, for example, English conscripts at the Battle of Hastings because, ever since King Alfred's day, all parts of the country had been required to produce a quota of fighting men for the *Fyrd* as this general levy was called. King Alfred had cleverly made all his subjects soldiers. He had also divided the country into military districts and required every owner of five hides of land or more, to do thane's service. This entailed them serving throughout a particular campaign, getting to the field of battle under their own steam, and even providing their own chain mail and weapons! Perhaps that is the original reason why the British as a race have always disliked the idea of any form of compulsory military service, and such pleasantaries as the press-gangs of the 18th century did nothing to alter these views. It was not until the wars of this century, that the sheer size of the global conflicts made it necessary to provide enormous numbers of men (and women), not only to do the fighting, but also to undertake the other hundred and one jobs necessary for success in modern warfare. Even then there was not an immediate introduction of conscription, because of the tremendous surge of patriotism at the beginning of World War I. This led thousands of men to volunteer to fight for King and Country. So it was not until January 1916, when this stream of volunteers had all but dried up, that the Military Service Act was passed and a call-up was introduced.

This state of affairs was not repeated at the start of World War II. The war was only a few hours old, when Parliament passed the National Service (Armed Forces) Act, which made all physically fit males between the ages of 18 and 41 liable to military service. This was the first legislation and it was followed in 1941, by another Act which extended the upper age limit for men to 51 and also made women liable for military service. In fact, only a few men over 41 were ever conscripted and none over 45. By the end of 1939, 727,000 men had been registered; in 1940 the figure was 4,100,000; and in 1941 a further 2,222,000 were called up. From then on the numbers dropped sharply, as the only eligible men left were those in reserved occupations, plus each new generation as it reached the minimum call-up age. The Armed Forces, which in 1938 had numbered only 381,000, rose after only one year of war to $2\frac{1}{4}$ million, and by D-Day, June 1944, nearly one third of the entire male population of working age, were serving in the Forces. By April 1945, the British Forces had reached a peak of just under five million, three million of whom were in the Army. Conscription was accepted as being all very necessary for global war, but what about peacetime? Would the end of World War II bring with it the end of conscription? World events, in the shape of the steadily worsening international situation which has become known as the 'Cold War', combined with Britain's world-wide Commonwealth and Empire commitments, prevented this from happening for a further 18 years. As far as actual

Left: The artist Malcolm Greensmith told me that this was almost a self portrait, because he did his initial training with the 16/5 Lancers at Waitwith Lines, Catterick Camp — hence the label on the trunk which is addressed to CO 16/5 Lancers. He was conscripted in May 1957 and after passing out from Catterick, did the rest of his two years' service with the 3rd Carabiniers (Prince of Wales's) Dragoon Guards, known normally as just the '3 DG' now amalgamated with the Royal Scots Greys to form The Royal Scots Dragoon Guards (Carabiniers and Greys). Malcolm has used his own army number on the regulation fibre suitcase on which the tired trooper is resting his elbow. *Adam Forty*

legislation was concerned, there was a gap of some three years after the end of the war, before the 1948 National Service Acts were passed by Parliament. These remained in force until the call-up was ended on 31 December 1960. Despite this, the very last National Servicemen did not leave the Army until the early summer of 1963. I have chosen to concentrate in this book on the period 1948 to 1963, and have done this deliberately, not because I wish to deny for one moment the wonderful job done by National Servicemen before 1948 — let's face it they won the war! — but merely because it enables me to keep the book down to manageable proportions. I have also deliberately concentrated on the Army, the Royal Navy and Royal Air Force deserving their own special record.

The 1948 Act, which was effective from 1 January 1949, fixed a limit to the length of National Service for the first time, before then it had merely been a nebulous arrangement that you would be kept for as long as your services were required. Now, all National Servicemen had to serve for 18 months full time service, followed by four years part time service with the reserves, that is to say, the Territorial Army. The Act also did away with such niceties as demob suits and gratuities. Later in 1950, full time service was lengthened to two years, but the period of part-time service was reduced accordingly, so that the total was still $5\frac{1}{2}$ years. This was in line with the experience of other countries, that two years was the optimum period for full time service in those days. (It is interesting to note that nowadays the NATO nations which have kept National Service have generally reduced their full time service commitment to under two years, the periods ranging down to as little as nine months, whilst the Warsaw Pact nations have generally kept theirs at two years. A further interesting statistic is that 10 of the 15 NATO nations have kept National Service, whilst *all* the Warsaw Pact nations have kept it.) All young men between the ages of 18 and 26 were liable to National Service, the only automatic exceptions being those in government posts abroad, mental defectives, blind persons, or members of the clergy. Certain trades were classified as *Reserved Occupations*. and provided a young man stayed at work in one of them, then he was exempt from military service. These occupations included coalminer, underground oil shale worker, merchant seaman, seagoing fisherman, agricultural worker in essential food production, graduate science teacher and police cadet. It was also possible to delay doing one's National Service, by obtaining *deferment*. This was permitted to allow a young man to complete his apprenticeship or finish his education at, for example, a university. Deferment was initially limited to a maximum of eight years to cover the long training needed to become a doctor or a dentist. Later this period was extended to 12 and then to 18 years.

Numbers involved

From the first conscription in 1939 until it ended in 1960, 3,800,000 men were called up for the Army, compared with one million for the RAF and half a million for the Royal Navy. If one takes just one year as an example, and I have chosen 1953, the year in which the Korean War ended, there were 286,000 men registered and of these 160,000 were drafted into the Armed Forces or entered as volunteers. The remaining 126,000 were broken down as follows: medically unfit: 41,500; available but still awaiting medical inspection: 10,600; awaiting a decision on deferment: 900; deferred apprentices: 31,700; post apprenticeships: 400; training for professional qualifications (eg: articled pupils): 6,400; farm workers: 5,800; coalminers: 11,000; seamen and fishermen: 5,200; university students and student teachers: 10,400; abroad, including emigrants: 800; all others (including conscientious objectors, hardship cases etc): 1,300. Looking at these figures one can see that, whilst the number of conscientious objectors must have been very small indeed, nearly half of those registered had valid reasons for not doing their National Service immediately.

Medical and choice of job

After registering, the young hopeful normally had to wait about two weeks before receiving a notice asking him to report for a medical examination. I say 'asking', but of course it was mandatory, and those who decided not to attend, did

Both: Soldier

Above: 'X' marks probably the most well known National Serviceman, Leslie Thomas, whose books have sold in their millions. His entry in *Who's Who* contains the item: 'Army Service 1949-51. Rose to Lance-Corporal'. 'That,' says the author of *The Virgin Soldiers*, 'just about sums it up. When I went to sign on for National Service I was a young journalist and I told the Labour Exchange clerk that I was a "junior reporter". Whether through oversight or downright malice, I don't know, but he entered "junior porter" on the form. I wondered why I spent so much of my army service carrying heavy loads about!' While he was serving in Signapore the length of service was increased from 18 months to two years. 'The Army and I were not very happy together,' he recalls, but thinking of his best seller, he added: 'But it's been very good to me since.' *Leslie Thomas*

so at the risk of being fined £100 and, worse still, being imprisoned for up to two years. Like all terms of imprisonment during an individual's National Service, this did not count towards the total service period of $5\frac{1}{2}$ years. I will not dwell on the subject of these medical inspections, but those who attended will probably be able to remember the 'ritual' of their own in graphic detail. Mine, although it was in wartime and thus not strictly within the compass of this book, was undoubtedly very much like all the rest. That all important 'sample' was produced with or without effort, the magic 'cough' routine was duly complied with, and various parts of one's anatomy were struck by that strange little rubber hammer. In his book, which contains the fascinating reminscences of 24 National Servicemen, and is entitled appropriately 'All Bull', B. S. Johnson explains how some drama students, including Peter O'Toole, used to give classes on how to fail the medical: '. . . aided by too much alcohol, too little food and sleep.' On the same day as the medical the 18-year old would also have a talk with the Military Interviewing Officer. He was usually a retired senior officer, who spent some time and effort explaining the role of the individual Services to each man, and telling him a little about the various branches within the three Services. Together they would then try to select the most appropriate military job to suit the particular talents of the young man in question. Unfortunately, the actual allocation system was far more impersonal than perhaps this interview suggested, and inevitably by 'Sod's Law', large a number of those interviewed were called up into an entirely different Service or branch to the one they had so carefully selected! Getting round pegs into round holes, was, however, one of the main preoccupations of the Services at that time, so as not to waste the individual talents of the recruits. The Personnel Selection Officer (PSO), who carried out an even more detailed assessment once the young man had reached his Primary Training Centre, was ususally far more successful, but by then of course the damage might have already been done and the expert, highly trained chef would find himself destined to repair tank engines, whilst the skilled motor mechanic stirred the Brown Windsor. A month to six weeks after the medical, an enlistment notice (see photograph) would arrive, telling each man when and where to report, sending him a railway warrant and an advance of pay, together with lots of useful information. This included a reminder to explain the situation to his employer, who was required by law to keep his job open for him and to take him back after National Service for a minimum of six months. The authorities tried to be humane about the issue of these notices, giving every man ample time to settle his private affairs before 'The Big Day'. To the Army, National Service at its peak meant thousands of young men arriving on its doorsteps every fortnight, 23 times a year — there were two drafts each month except for December, when there was only one for obvious reasons. All these new arrivals had to be received, documented, kitted out, fed, housed, taught the rudiments of drill and other basic military skills, and got as physically fit as possible, during the all too brief weeks at their respective Primary Training Centres. 'It is outrageous that the youth of today should be subject to this tedious, squalid and regimented discharge of an imaginary duty', so wrote the late Gilbert Harding. I personally feel that his remarks, if one considers the Army as a whole, are a little unfair and uncalled for, however, they do perhaps contain more than a grain of truth if applied to those first hectic and traumatic days, when the bemused arrivals rapidly discovered that they were there primarily to learn not to think for themselves, but rather to obey orders without question at all times! Basic training had of necessity to be a shock treatment, but I don't think it did the vast majority of the new arrivals any harm at all (except to their dignity) to be shaken out of their civvy street lethargy and made to jump to it! Of course there were ogres among the staff of these initial training centres, those who took a savage delight in making life as bloody as possible for the new arrivals, delighting in causing both mental and bodily anguish to those unfortunates who unwittingly offended them. However, despite what one is inclined to surmise from most of the books and films about the British Army of that era, I do think that they were in the minority. Some poor unfortunates were undoubtedly driven to the end of their tether, but the proportion of such brutality was relatively small as compared with the large number of well run and humane establishments, where the permanent staff tried their best to help the new arrivals to became acclimatised to the strangeness of the new life as quickly and as painlessly as possible. Coming from a boarding school I personally found Army life a sheer delight! The freedom from petty regulations (!), being able to smoke, or talk to girls without being beaten for it, and of receiving far more money than ever before — and that was in the days when a private solider received three shillings a day, a small fortune to someone who had existed on one shilling and sixpence pocket money a week! Above all, the pleasure of feeling really fit and alive, made up for all the hardships of communal life and wearing a unifrom, which one was used to anyway. Someone who hadn't experienced the 'delights' of boarding school, or had the worry of leaving a wife and family with little money coming in, probably found the transitional period far more difficult, but at least everyone had the consolation of knowing that they were all in the same boat. As an article in *Soldier* magazine of January 1963 explained: '. . . with the hard beds, early rising, the kit, the rumours, the dictatorial

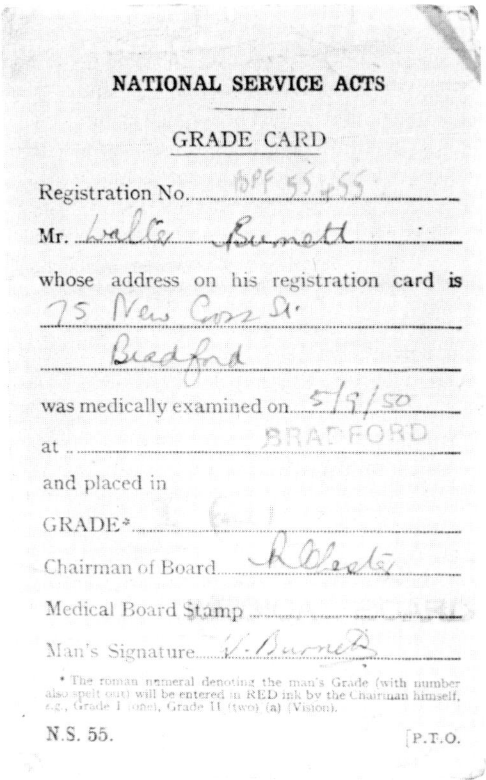

NATIONAL SERVICE ACTS

GRADE CARD

Registration No. ....

Mr. ....

whose address on his registration card is

....

....

was medically examined on 5/9/50

at BRADFORD

and placed in

GRADE* ....

Chairman of Board ....

Medical Board Stamp ....

Man's Signature ....

* The roman numeral denoting the man's Grade (with number also spelt out) will be entered in RED ink by the Chairman himself, e.g., Grade I (one), Grade II (two) (a) (Vision).

N.S. 55. [P.T.O.

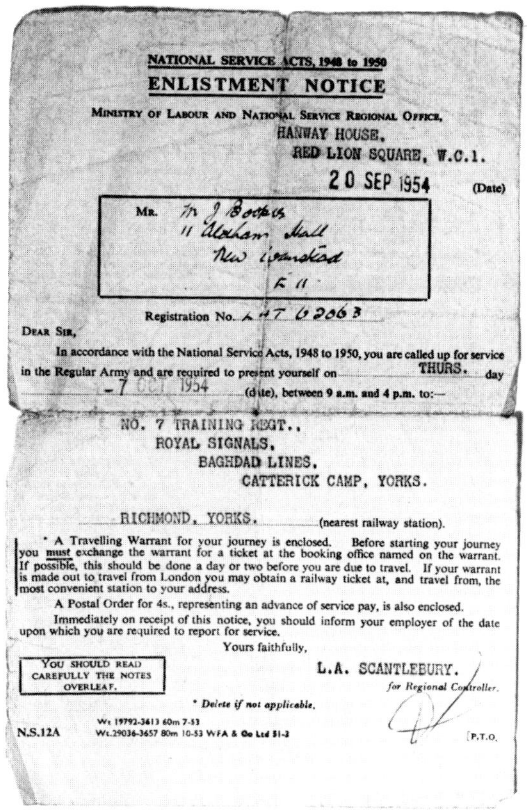

NATIONAL SERVICE ACTS, 1948 to 1950

ENLISTMENT NOTICE

MINISTRY OF LABOUR AND NATIONAL SERVICE REGIONAL OFFICE,
HANWAY HOUSE,
RED LION SQUARE, W.C.1.

20 SEP 1954 (Date)

MR. ....

Registration No. ....

DEAR SIR,

In accordance with the National Service Acts, 1948 to 1950, you are called up for service in the Regular Army and are required to present yourself on THURS. day 7 OCT 1954 (date), between 9 a.m. and 4 p.m. to:—

NO. 7 TRAINING REGT.,
ROYAL SIGNALS,
BAGHDAD LINES,
CATTERICK CAMP, YORKS.

RICHMOND, YORKS. (nearest railway station).

* A Travelling Warrant for your journey is enclosed. Before starting your journey you must exchange the warrant for a ticket at the booking office named on the warrant. If possible, this should be done a day or two before you are due to travel. If your warrant is made out to travel from London you may obtain a railway ticket at, and travel from, the most convenient station to your address.

A Postal Order for 4s., representing an advance of service pay, is also enclosed.

Immediately on receipt of this notice, you should inform your employer of the date upon which you are required to report for service.

Yours faithfully,

L.A. SCANTLEBURY.
for Regional Controller.

YOU SHOULD READ CAREFULLY THE NOTES OVERLEAF.

* *Delete if not applicable.*

N.S.12A Wt 19792-3613 60m 7-53 Wt.29036-3657 80m 10-53 WFA & Co Ltd 51-3 [P.T.O.

Far left: Grade Card. After the medical, each man was issued with a grading card showing his medical category. *Adam Forty*

Left: Enlistment Notice. Five or six weeks after his medical, the young potential recruit would receive his 'call-up papers', which included this enlistment notice. (Original kindly lent to me by Michael Booker.) *Adam Forty*

corporal (what an exalted rank that seemed at first) and most of all the feeling from the time he is alloted it, just a number, the National Serviceman at first found Army life just too much for him. Yet through it all there was the knowledge that everyone else was in the same boat and the problems, so shared, diminished. When the first ten days or so — they seemed like months — had passed, and the Army felt that its new recruits were just about fit to be let out of camp in the Queen's uniform, friends had been made and Army life became a little more tolerable. Later it became clear that early misgivings could be simply blamed on changing to a new way of life. Once the adjustment was made the bright young National Serviceman made friends with the Army and took the same pride in its traditions as the Regular soldier. Whilst, for some, National Service remained simply an intrusion on their life, for most, who accepted it as a duty to their country, it was a wonderful opportunity. Here were two years in which to do something quite different and see something of the world. For many wise young men it provided a breathing space in which to take stock of their lives. For those who had found themselves in the wrong job after leaving school, here was the chance to make the break and work towards a new career. . . . '

That may be a little oversimplified and starry-eyed view of a National Serviceman's life but it is on the whole a fair one. I will not attempt here to outline the everyday life of the average National Serviceman in the Army, because that is exactly the purpose of my complete book. They say that actions speak louder than words, so hopefully the pictures I have managed to collect will remind those who were National Servicemen what it was like. Perhaps they will also serve to give the present generation an insight into how different their lives might have been had not the decision been made to go for an all volunteer force. The Sandys White Paper of 1957 was the document that sealed the demise of National Service, announcing the Government's intention to build up the Regular Army and to depend on a highly mobile strategic reserve, rather than maintaining vast, expensive to run, static overseas garrisons. It was probably the biggest change of British military policy ever made in modern times. A further White Paper (Cmnd 175 of May 1957) explained how it was hoped that, in its death throes, National Service would become more selective, as regular recruiting improved and the Army's worldwide commitments reduced. Fortunately the planners had the good sense to preface their remarks with a paragraph in which they explained that the decision to end National Service had been taken against this optimistic background, however, they added: '. . . if this expectation should be falsified by events, Parliament would have to consider the action to be taken'. 'The best laid schemes o' mice an' men, Gang aft a-gley' and trouble in Aden, Brunei and Sarawak, plus a slightly slower than anticipated increase in regular recruiting, resulted in the inevitable happening, and National Servicemen in the last few intakes, found themselves having to stay on for a further six months.

I doubt if many will realise that conscription, even during the war, did not apply to Northern Ireland. The Army tried to keep the Northern Irish regiments up to scratch with Irishmen who were living in this country, or from men of Irish extraction, or from volunteers from Northern Ireland, who could and did, sign on for two years service if they wished. So the happy mixture of men from all over the United Kingdom was maintained, as was the mixing of all classes of society. Usually, however, those who had received a better education were inevitably needed as potential officers and NCOs, but by no means all of these had the necessary qualities of leadership, and some were perfectly satisfied to serve out their time in the ranks. I have covered the very special part played by the National Service OCTUs (Officer Cadet Training Units) in this book, and it is worth remembering that National Service officers proved their ability all over the world, and did so with great bravery and courage. 2-Lt William Purves, for example, formerly a bank clerk in Kelso, made history by being the only National Serviceman to be awarded the Distinguished Service Order for exceptional bravery and leadership in Korea in November 1951, whilst serving with 1 KOSB. In Palestine, Korea, Malaya, Cyprus, the Canal Zone, Kenya and all the other 'trouble spots', young National Servicemen proved their courage and 395 were killed in action — 'too young to vote, but old enough to kill and to be killed', as it has been somewhat cynically expressed.

Was it all worthwhile?

One of the major questions about National Service which must be asked is was it all worthwhile? As I have already tried to explain, from the individual's point of view the truthful answer to this question is bound to be mixed. For some it was a complete waste of time, for others a wonderful experience, not to have been missed. An unofficial survey which was quoted in an article in the 1956 edition of *Brassey's Annual* said that 15% seemed to like the life, 10% really hated every minute of it (and in consequence were thoroughly bad soldiers), whilst the remaining 75% were lukewarm and looked forward eagerly to the day their full time service would end. However, this last group still did their job to the best of their abilities, and tried to remain as cheerful as they could. It was certainly easier for them to remain interested and cheerful if they felt that they were doing a proper job of work which was of value to the Army and to their country. So morale was higher among those National Servicemen serving overseas, especially when they were on active service, whilst those doing boring administrative jobs in camps back in England, were the really discontented ones. Pointless 'bullshit', such as whitewashing stones around the camp perimeter, cutting the grass between the huts with nail scissors, scrubbing out coal buckets, only to see them filled with coal as soon as they were finished, all these sorts of asinine and thoroughly pointless tasks, were the stuff of the many stories that one now sees so often quoted about National Service being a complete waste of time. Necessary fatigues, even the inevitable 'spud bashing' were in general done with good humoured resignation as at least there was some point to them. The scores of ex-National Servicemen who have written to me in the preparation of this book have naturally been mainly from the group who enjoyed their service, otherwise they logically would not have made the effort. They, at least, clearly enjoyed themselves and now look back on it with feelings of warmth and nostalgia for the places they visited, the good friends they made and the good times they had.

However, with the greatest respect to all of them, National Service was not instituted to be fun for the men concerned, not to provide a magic carpet to exotic faraway places. It was a vital part of the British nation's contribution to maintaining the often rickety peace that has prevailed ever since the end of World War 2. And make no bones about it, the avowed intention of Communism was and still is, world domination, by fair means or foul, and without National Service, we could never have started to meet our widespread commitments, especially with the continual internal problems which the breakup of the British Empire brought along in its wake. Malaya is a perfect example: A relatively small number of Communist insurgents caused widespread havoc by murder, sabotage and terrorism, necessitating the employment of a large number of British and Commonwealth troops for 12 long and difficult years. National Servicemen did their fair share in accounting for the large number of insurgents who were killed during the Malayan Emergency. Another notable group of National Servicemen, some 2,000 in all, went to serve in Hong Kong and then carved out their own special place in history, as members of 27th Infantry Brigade (called by some the 'Woolworth Brigade') who were the first British formation to fight in Korea. These youngsters in such battalions as the Middlesex, the Argyll and Sutherland Highlanders and the King's Own Scottish Borderers, were the first to join the United Nations forces in their struggle against Communism in Korea. In a splendid open letter at Christmas 1951, to the mother of one of these young National Servicemen (a Private Sammy Wilson of 1 KOSB) the well known correspondent Arthur Helliwell of the *People* explained graphically what it was like to be a National Serviceman serving in Korea, and how Sammy and his mates refused to be downhearted '... still wearing a smile, that would gladden your heart if you could see it ...'. And of course the same cheerfulness and high morale applied to those National Servicemen fighting the EOKA terrorists in Cyprus, the Mau-Mau killers in Kenya and all the rest. The answer to the question posed at the beginning of this paragraph must undoubtedly be a resounding 'Yes' from the point of view of the Army and the country as a whole, National Service *was* worth all the heartaches — indeed the Army could never have managed all its commitments without their invaluable assistance. And let's face it, that is really the acid test, the individual's feelings must on such occasions be subjugated to the requirements of his country. With typical Whitehall cunning, the Services were also able to get this invaluable assistance at cut rate, it being (in 1960) four times cheaper to pay a National Serviceman than a regular and twice as cheap to keep him, according to figures published in the *Economist* in December 1960.

But National Service really did more than just enable the British Army to fulfil its commitments. Conscription put a wonderful cross-section of characters into khaki — from public schoolboys headed for top jobs in industry and commerce, to ambitious young mechanics, and artisans; from professional sportsmen, doctors, dentists etc, to unskilled labourers, spivs, even burglars and layabouts, they were all conscripted into the Army and, as *Soldier* put it: '... each one playing his part in watching over the interests of his home and country, each one coming to terms with Army life in his own way, and leaving his mark. Without him the Army will never be quite the same again.'

The chapters of this book need little further written explanation, so apart from some longish captions, I have let the photographs tell the story of what it was like to be called up, given basic military training, and then learn an Army trade. This is followed by a brief look at the methods of trooping, including a sentimental glimpse at the ss *Vienna*, which was one of the small troop ferries which used to chug between Harwich and the Hook of Holland — I vividly remember the last time I travelled on this route as we ran aground before even leaving the Hook ('something wrong with the steering' was the official excuse, but all the troops onboard were convinced that the captain was stoned out of his mind!) — we made it home in time for Christmas Eve, so that particular story had a happy ending. A round-up of jobs in units, the vital subjects of food, bedspaces and off duty pursuits are covered, as well as the more serious stuff of soldiering such as parades, exercises and operations. I have even included photographic evidence that some NCOs and

WOs really were human beings despite what many have thought to the contrary. The book closes with demobilisation and although I have been unsuccessful in obtaining photographs of the very last National Servicemen to leave the Army, at least I have managed to get a photo of the last National Serviceman who served in the Royal Military Police and left suitably handcuffed.

I have not included any pictures of part time service with the Territorial Army for a number of reasons, the main one being that as I was a TA Adjutant during the period in question (1954-56), I know from personal experience how much the average National Serviceman disliked their part-time service and what lengths we had to go to just to ensure that they carried out their statutory commitments. More importantly, I know how much harm it did to the TA, which was then and always will be, firmly rooted in the principles of voluntary service, so that any sort of compulsion of this kind was an anathema to any self-respecting Terrier.

I do hope that this book will give the reader as much fun as it has given me collecting the photographs and corresponding with the large number of ex-National Servicemen who have been kind enough to bare their souls in public. Thank you all for your help and cooperation.

Acknowledgements

I would like to thank many people for their help and advice during the preparation of this book and for providing me with so many marvellous photographs. First and foremost I must thank the editor and staff of *Soldier* magazine, for allowing me to use so many of their photographs and for their continual help. We in the British Army are exceedingly fortunate to have had such an excellent and devoted organisation 'Keeping the British Army in the Public Eye' ever since the end of World War II. Their attractive, readable and well illustrated magazine has month by month highlighted military matters for many years now, always maintaining the highest and most professional possible standards. I am personally very grateful for everything they have done — long may they continue to do it!

Secondly, I must thank my son Adam for taking so much trouble on my behalf with such excellent results — it is very nice to have a good photographer in the family! I would also like to thank the following:

Service and Civilian organisations

Photographic Department, Imperial War Museum; Royal Artillery Institution; Miss Daniell's Soldiers' Home; *Radio Times* Hulton Picture Library; Ministry of Defence Library; Royal Corps of Transport Museum; Royal Army Ordnance Corps Museum; *Western Mail & Echo* Ltd; Pan Books Ltd; *Bradford Telegraph & Argus*; Army Sports Control Board; Regular Commissions Board, Westbury; Welch Regiment Museum; Services Kinema Corporation; Womens' Royal Voluntary Service; National Council of the YMCA; British Red Cross Society; Rustcraft Cards; Army Search; Yorkshire County Cricket Club; Combined Services Entertainment Unit; Sandes Soldiers' & Airmen's Homes; NAAFI; Toc H; TANK Museum; Guards Depot; Royal British Legion; *Yorkshire Post*; *TAVR Magazine*; RAMC Historical Museum; ARMY Public Relations.

Individuals

W. Ashby; Lt-Col A. J. Barker; M. J. Booker; A. D. Barrowcliff (photos of L Cpl Swaysland); Sgt A. R. Bleese, RMP; W. Burnett; T. Coleman; G. Francis; R. J. Hale; E. I. Hatton; Rev D. C. Hodgson; J. R. Humphreys; P. Jackson; Lt-Col P. Love; D. Lynch; J. Mann; D. Padgett; J. Pickles; D. Pilkington; P. Rafferty; Maj (QM) P. Fleur de Pledge; R. Rimmer; A. G. H. Sage; J. Scroby; R. J. Shears; E. J. Spurway; L. Thomas; N. J. Watson; A. Ward; R. G. White; R. Wingham.

Finally, may I especially thank Malcolm Greensmith for his kindness in allowing me to use his evocative painting of a browned off National Serviceman. Having spent quite a few hours on Darlington station myself, I know exactly how he felt!

Note

I feel that it would be only fair if I were to put: 'E&OE' somewhere in this book. I have done my level best to try to make sure that the photos do actually show National Servicemen at work and at play, however, this has been exceptionally difficult, albeit impossible, to check in some cases. Therefore, I cannot swear that there aren't any regular soldiers featured as well, because, after all, the whole of the British Army was a glorious mixture of Regular and National Service throughout the period I have covered. So, to any regular soldier who sees himself in these pages, I say: 'please excuse my error, but let's face it, you couldn't be in better company!'

Bradford, West Yorkshire
November 1979

George Forty

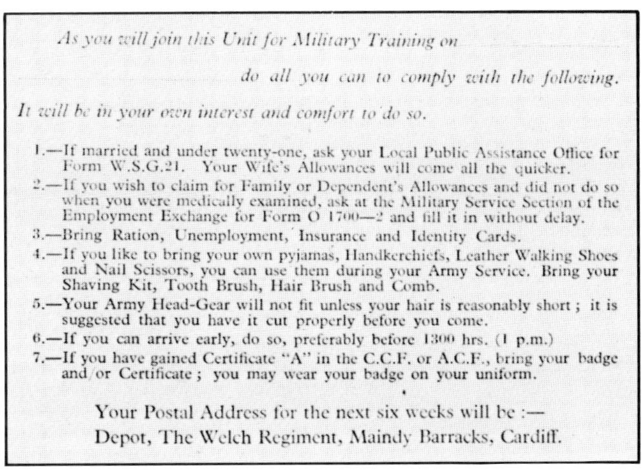

As you will join this Unit for Military Training on

do all you can to comply with the following.

It will be in your own interest and comfort to do so.

1.—If married and under twenty-one, ask your Local Public Assistance Office for Form W.S.G.21. Your Wife's Allowances will come all the quicker.
2.—If you wish to claim for Family or Dependent's Allowances and did not do so when you were medically examined, ask at the Military Service Section of the Employment Exchange for Form O 1700—2 and fill it in without delay.
3.—Bring Ration, Unemployment, Insurance and Identity Cards.
4.—If you like to bring your own pyjamas, Handkerchiefs, Leather Walking Shoes and Nail Scissors, you can use them during your Army Service. Bring your Shaving Kit, Tooth Brush, Hair Brush and Comb.
5.—Your Army Head-Gear will not fit unless your hair is reasonably short; it is suggested that you have it cut properly before you come.
6.—If you can arrive early, do so, preferably before 1300 hrs. (1 p.m.)
7.—If you have gained Certificate "A" in the C.C.F. or A.C.F., bring your badge and/or Certificate; you may wear your badge on your uniform.

Your Postal Address for the next six weeks will be :—
Depot, The Welch Regiment, Maindy Barracks, Cardiff.

Right: Some units sent their own 'Greetings Cards' to National Servicemen — note item 5!
Adam Forty

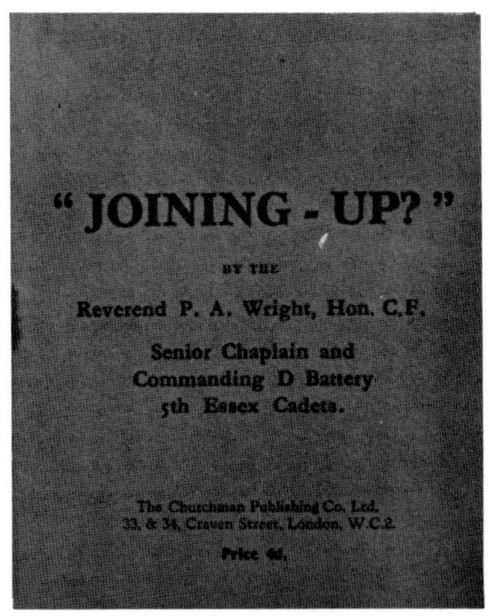

Far right: This little booklet entitled 'JOINING-UP?' contained lots of helpful hints and the inevitable dire warnings about the evils of drink and 'Good Time Girls'.
Adam Forty

Those first few days

The Day arrived all too quickly. Family goodbyes were normally said at the local station, then that rather apprehensive journey to some faraway centre of military culture like Aldershot or Catterick, and your service had really begun!

Below: Once you arrived at your destination, you were met by a kindly (?) sergeant who helped you on to the back of a TCV (troop carrying vehicle — usually a 3-tonner with fold-up seats along the sides). This particular intake of recruits being met at Aldershot station, was bound for the 1st Training Battalion, RAOC, on 4 March 1948, and was their first complete National Service intake. *RAOC Museum*

Right: Unit clerks interviewed each new arrival, allocated such basic things as Army Numbers and prepared their AB64 Part I. *RAOC Museum*

Below right: Army Book 64. That precious little brown covered book, which stayed with you throughout your National Service, was a most treasured possession, because it contained a record of everything you did *and* more importantly, formed your means of identity — can't you just hear that burly MP asking: 'Where's your AB 64 lad?' Doesn't it still send a little shiver down your back? Part 2 was your pay book in which all debits and credits were noted down. *Adam Forty*

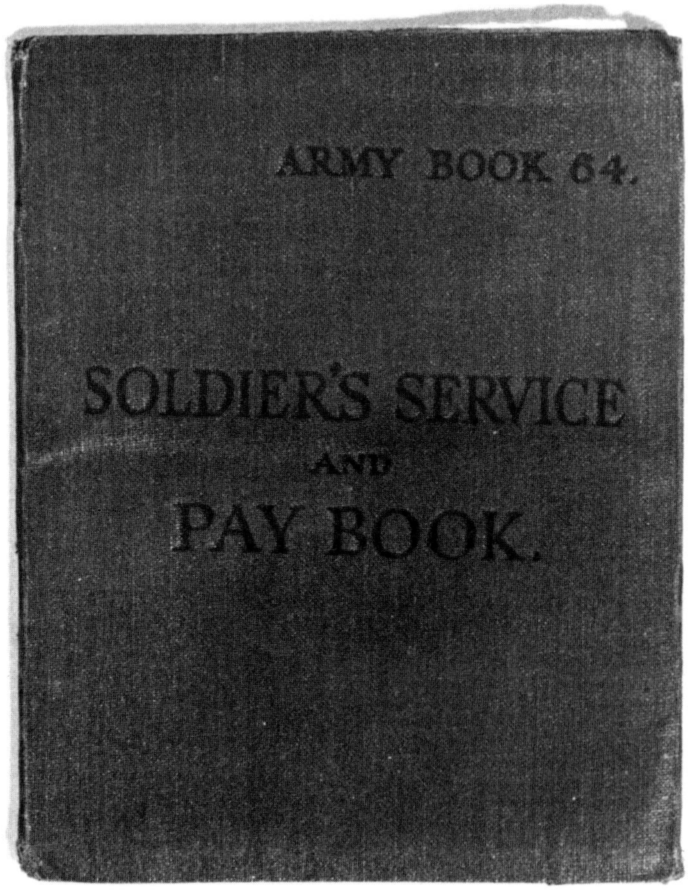

Above: There was of course a lot more arrival documentation. Here RAOC platoon officers withdraw ration books, sweet coupons, clothing coupons etc, Aldershot, March 1948. *RAOC Museum*

Left: Then it was off to the Quartermaster's Stores for your kit. Here recruits collect, in bulk, all these items which didn't need to be tried on, such as webbing, cleaning kit, razors, 'housewives', etc, all packed in those unforgettable (and bloody heavy!) kitbags. *RAOC Museum*

Above: The moment had now arrived when you were to put on a uniform at last. 'You won't get a better fit at Burtons!' Welch Regiment recruits are kitted out by an ever smiling and generous Quartermaster.
Western Mail & Echo Ltd

Centre right: After the check fitting, NS men draw their hats, battledress, greatcoats and boots.
RAOC Museum

Below right: Then it's into the fitting room to try to sort the lot out. Goodbye civvies!
RAOC Museum

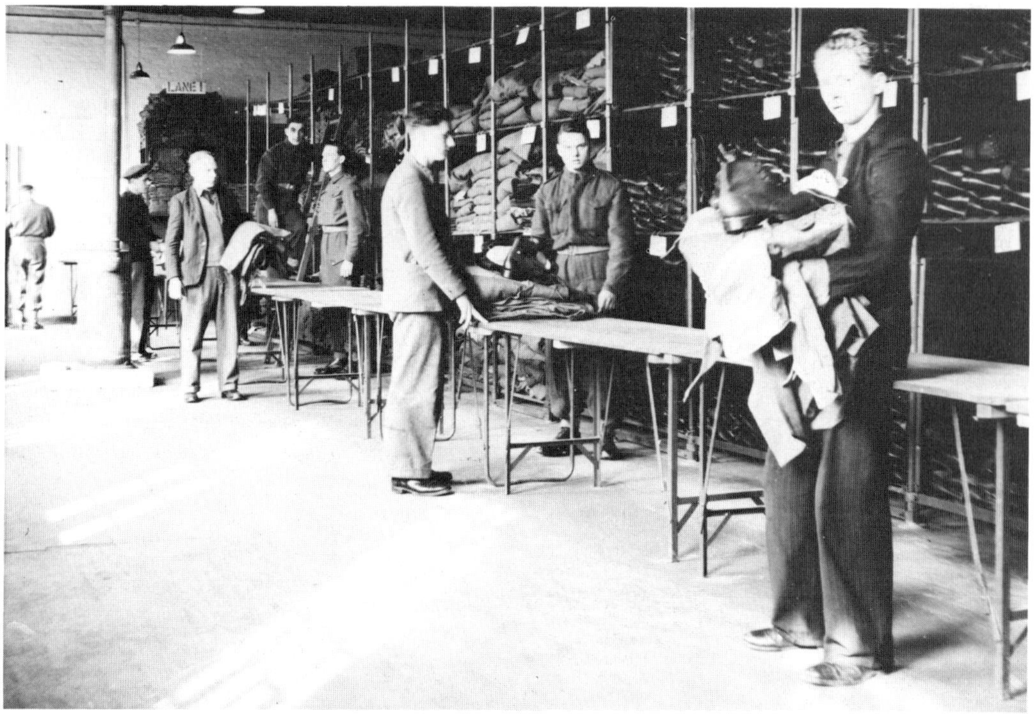

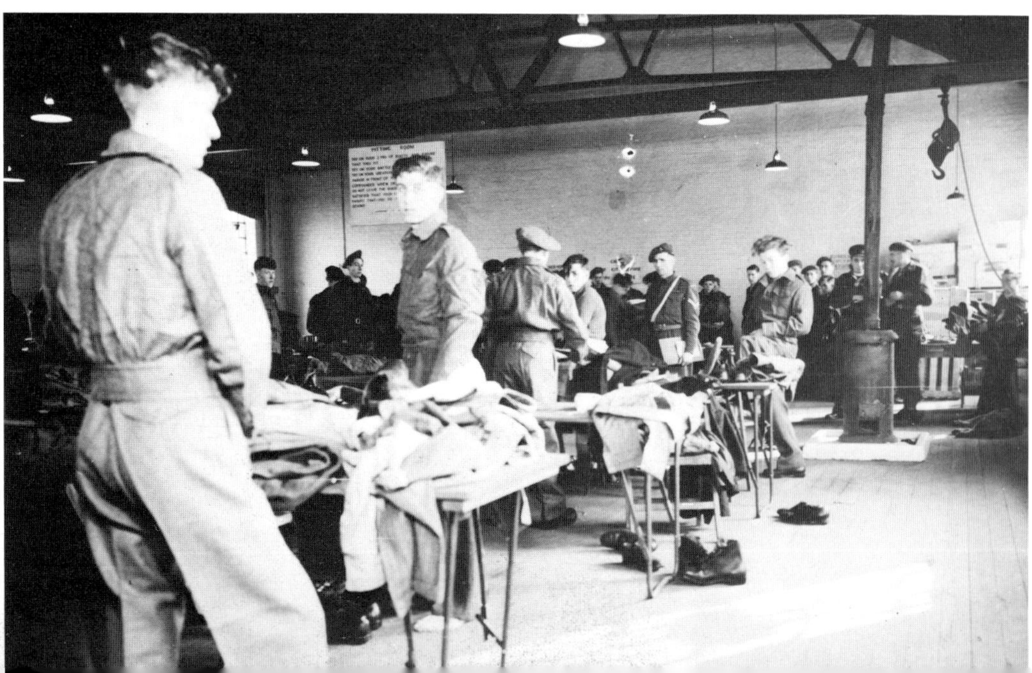

Left: Even wearing an Army uniform doesn't make some recruits look older — these 18-year olds were photographed by a *Picture Post* cameraman at the Royal West Kent Depot Maidstone, 13 November 1954.
Radio Times Hulton Picture Library

Below: Goodbye to all that! One of the first things they did was to give you a haircut — whether you thought you needed one or not, hence the rather wistful expression on the face of the man in the 'hot seat'. When there wasn't a proper camp barber's shop, or they needed to speed up production, then they did the deed in the barrack room. Note the already shorn are getting on with cleaning their rifles.
Radio Times Hulton Picture Library

Right: Ouch! If I close my eyes I can still feel that needle!
Radio Times Hulton Picture Library

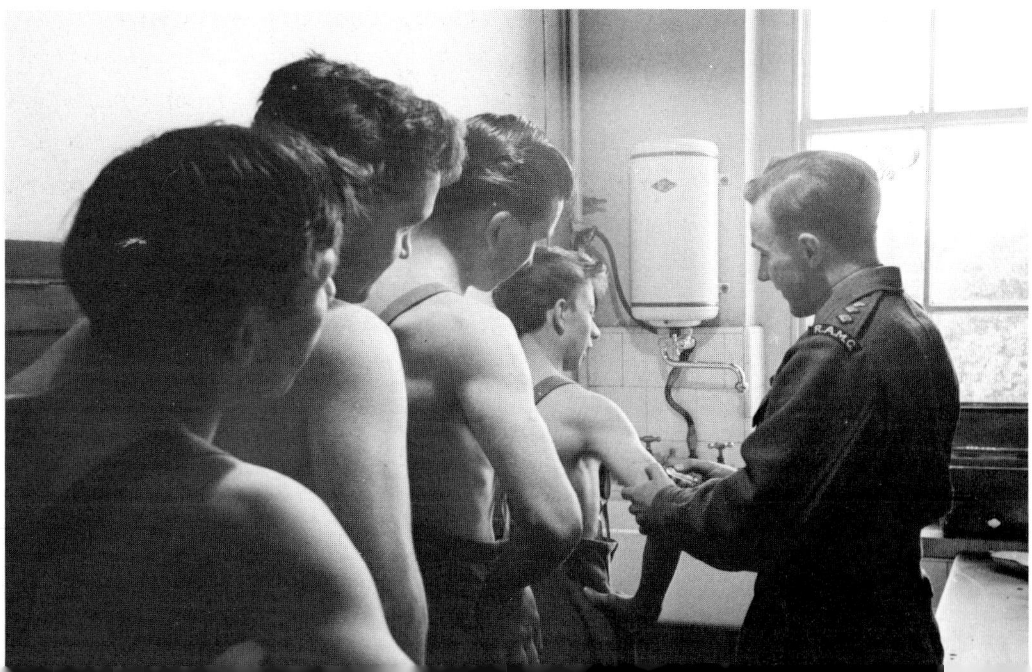

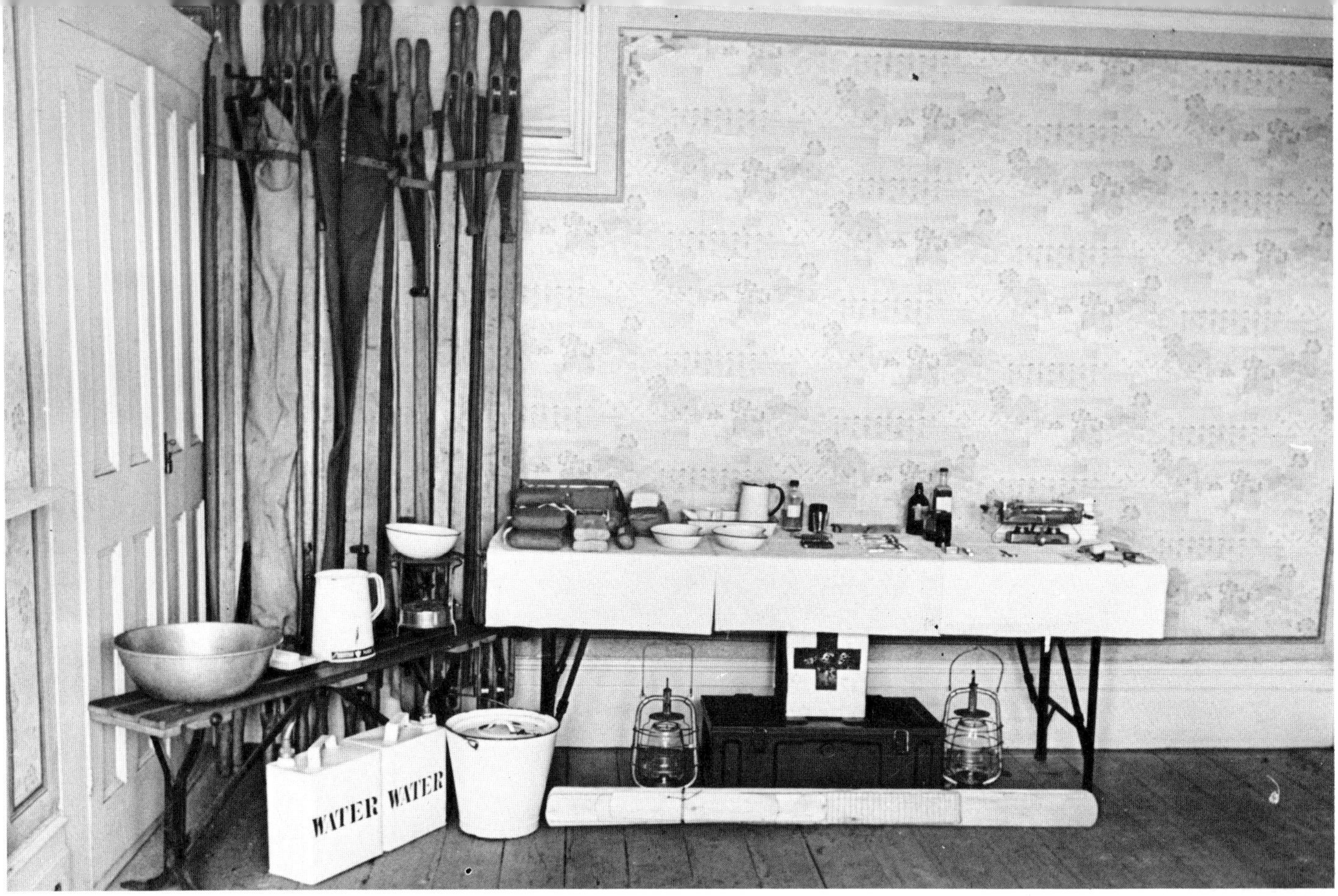

Above: Why did MI Rooms, which were supposed to be places of succour and comfort, always look so bloody spartan and uncomfortable? *RCT Museum*

Right: Of course if you happened to be a well known celebrity, then you were entitled to expect some 'red carpet' treatment. Dai Dower, the Welsh boxer, arrives at the barrack gates to a special welcome.
Syndication International Ltd

Basic Training

In the early days, National Servicemen usually spent their first six weeks at a Primary Training Centre, learning the basic arts of soldiering and getting fit. Later this basic training was carried out at the training regiments and depots where the new recruits would go on to learn their selected army trades. No matter where it was done, this training was for the most part drill, PT, basic small arms training and more and more drill. It was also the period when the recruit learned all about army discipline, 'bull', and other quaint army customs.

Left: How did the army turn a scruffy civilian, hands deep in pockets and a surly expression on his face, into 'Superman'? The first step in the transformation was called 'Basic Training'. *Soldier*

Below left: A soldier's best friend is not his mother but his rifle. Here Scots Guards recruits clean theirs under the watchful eye of the hut NCO.
Miss Daniell's Soldiers' Home

WELSH GUARDS

Left: 'Not too bad, put in more work on the uppers now that the toes are shiny'. A platoon officer critically examines a recruit's boots. *Soldier*

Below far left: 'That's better lad. Next time you clean 'em properly and you won't find yourself on jankers!' *Soldier*

Below left: How many hours did we all spend cleaning, polishing and putting on blanco? *Soldier*

Above: Fighting fit and fit to fight. Recruits at Maindy Barracks, Cardiff, just off for a little stroll in the country. *Western Mail & Echo Ltd*

Centre right: One also had to do some strange things with logs. *RA Institution*

Below right: 'Straighten those arms!' *Soldier*

Right: Basic weapon training was an important part of early training. Here a squad of young Guardsmen learn to strip and assemble a Bren gun. *Soldier*

Below: Learning how to salute officers was vital or one could easily find oneself on a fizzer. *Soldier*

Below right: Rinse that mug and plate and don't forget your eating irons. *Soldier*

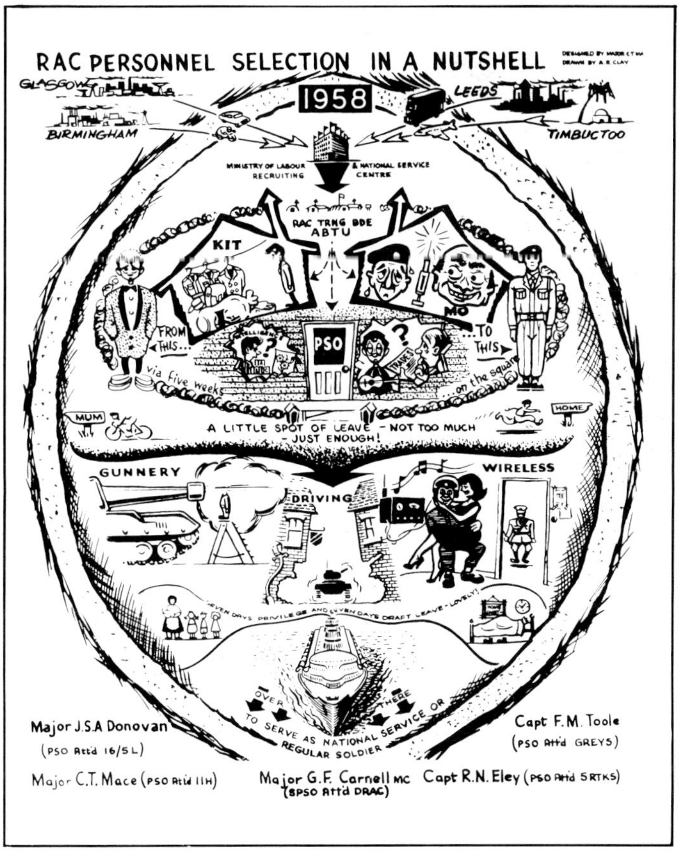

Top: 'Stand still you idle little men and don't anticipate the word of command!' Rifles at the slope, a squad of NS men of the Royal West Kent's Depot sample the delights of the drill square.
Radio Times Hulton Picture Library

Above: A quartet of perfect slopes as one might expect from the Guards.
Soldier

Right: RAC Personnel selection in a nutshell. The PSO tried his best, as this amusing cartoon shows. *Tank Museum*

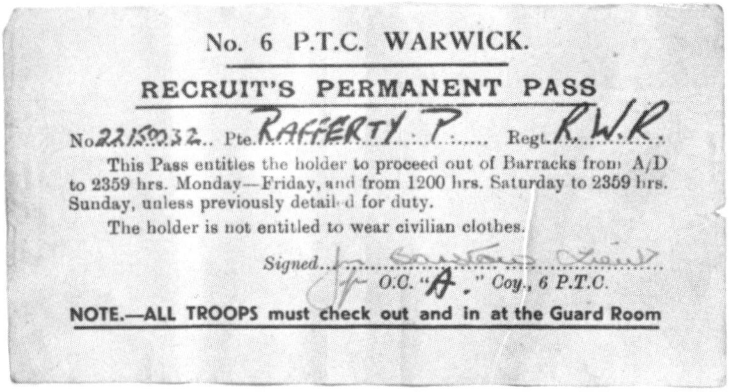

No. 6 P.T.C. WARWICK.

RECRUIT'S PERMANENT PASS

No 22150032 Pte. RAFFERTY P. Regt. R.W.R.

This Pass entitles the holder to proceed out of Barracks from A/D to 2359 hrs. Monday—Friday, and from 1200 hrs. Saturday to 2359 hrs. Sunday, unless previously detailed for duty.

The holder is not entitled to wear civilian clothes.

Signed .... Lieut
O.C. "A." Coy., 6 P.T.C.

NOTE.—ALL TROOPS must check out and in at the Guard Room

Top left: Once you had passed the first hurdle you might get a permanent pass like this one. *Adam Forty*

Above: But you still had to check out at the guardroom and that could be quite an ordeal! *Soldier*

Centre left: Having asked for photos of 'horrible sergeants' I was sent this one by ex-horrible sergeant R. J. Shears. I must admit that he looks much kinder than the ones I remember! He had an isolated detachment mainly composed of NS men at Houghton Camp, Dover, detached from No 46 Company RASC, Shorncliffe. He told me that he had found NS men much better soldiers than a lot of the 'demob-happy' men — which must account for his jolly smile. *R. J. Shears*

Below left: Who could fail but be reassured by the gentle, smiling countenance of this Guards provost sergeant! *Soldier*

Above right: All too quickly it was time to pass-off the square at the end of the basic training phase. Passing out parade at the Cardiff Primary Training Centre (PTC), July 1947. *T. Coleman*

Right: Photograph taken at the end of basic training, Royal Sussex Regiment Shorncliffe, 1947. *E. L. Rose*

Above: This early squad was at 96 PTC, Bodmin, Cornwall in August 1946. They are wearing the General Service cap badge. *Alan Sage*

Centre right: And after passing off the square the lucky ones would get a weekend pass. *Adam Forty*

Below right: Some Regimental Depots and Corps training establishments presented certificates, such as this one from the 'Dukes'. *Adam Forty*

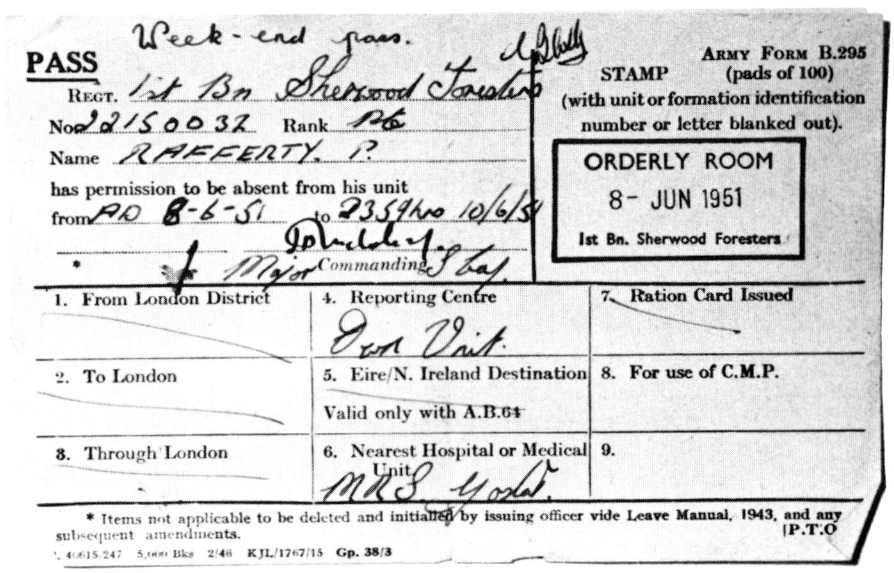

PASS Week-end pass.

ARMY FORM B.295 (pads of 100)

STAMP (with unit or formation identification number or letter blanked out).

ORDERLY ROOM
8- JUN 1951
1st Bn. Sherwood Foresters

REGT. 1st Bn Sherwood Foresters
No. 22150032 Rank Pte
Name RAFFERTY P.
has permission to be absent from his unit
from AD 8-6-51 to 2359hrs 10/6/51
* Major Commanding

1. From London District	4. Reporting Centre Own Unit	7. Ration Card Issued
2. To London	5. Eire/N. Ireland Destination Valid only with A.B.64	8. For use of C.M.P.
3. Through London	6. Nearest Hospital or Medical Unit MRS York	9.

* Items not applicable to be deleted and initialled by issuing officer vide Leave Manual, 1943, and any subsequent amendments.
P.T.O

40615/247 5,000 Bks 2/46 KJL/1767/15 Gp. 38/3

Certificate of Merit

This is to Certify that 23550034 SCROBY J. having completed his ten weeks Recruit Training at THE REGIMENTAL DEPOT THE DUKE OF WELLINGTON'S REGIMENT (West Riding) in an exemplary manner, having passed with merit all the tests required of him, and having maintained a high standard of efficiency, discipline and training throughout, has been nominated THE BEST RECRUIT of his platoon.

In recognition whereof this Certificate of Merit is awarded to him.

WELLESLEY BARRACKS, HALIFAX.

K G Exham. MAJOR GENERAL
Colonel, The Duke of Wellington's Regiment.

Learning a trade

Basic training was always followed by trade training, during which the now fairly well acclimatised recruits got down to learning the basics of their chosen trade — that is to say, the one selected for them by the Personnel Selection Officer (PSO), which was hopefully the one they wanted as well. The Army required an enormous number of different skills in addition to those of the infantryman and the other 'teeth arms', which were all vital to the smooth running of the whole team. So National Servicemen became tank crews, gun crews, engineers, signallers, truck drivers, storemen, medical orderlies, mechanics, cooks, pioneers and all the rest. The photos in this chapter show just a few of these trades being taught at various training regiments — the finished products are covered later.

Left: Learning to drive a Centurion tank. SSM Hillary, 9th Lancers, who earned a Military Medal at El Hamma, when his tank knocked out three enemy anti-tank guns, gives a recruit driver instructions on how to start up and move off, at the 57th Training Regiment RAC, Waithwith Lines, Catterick. *IWM*

Below left: No 149 Battery Continuation Troop on parade in the Gun Park at 64th Training Regiment, RA. *RA Institution*

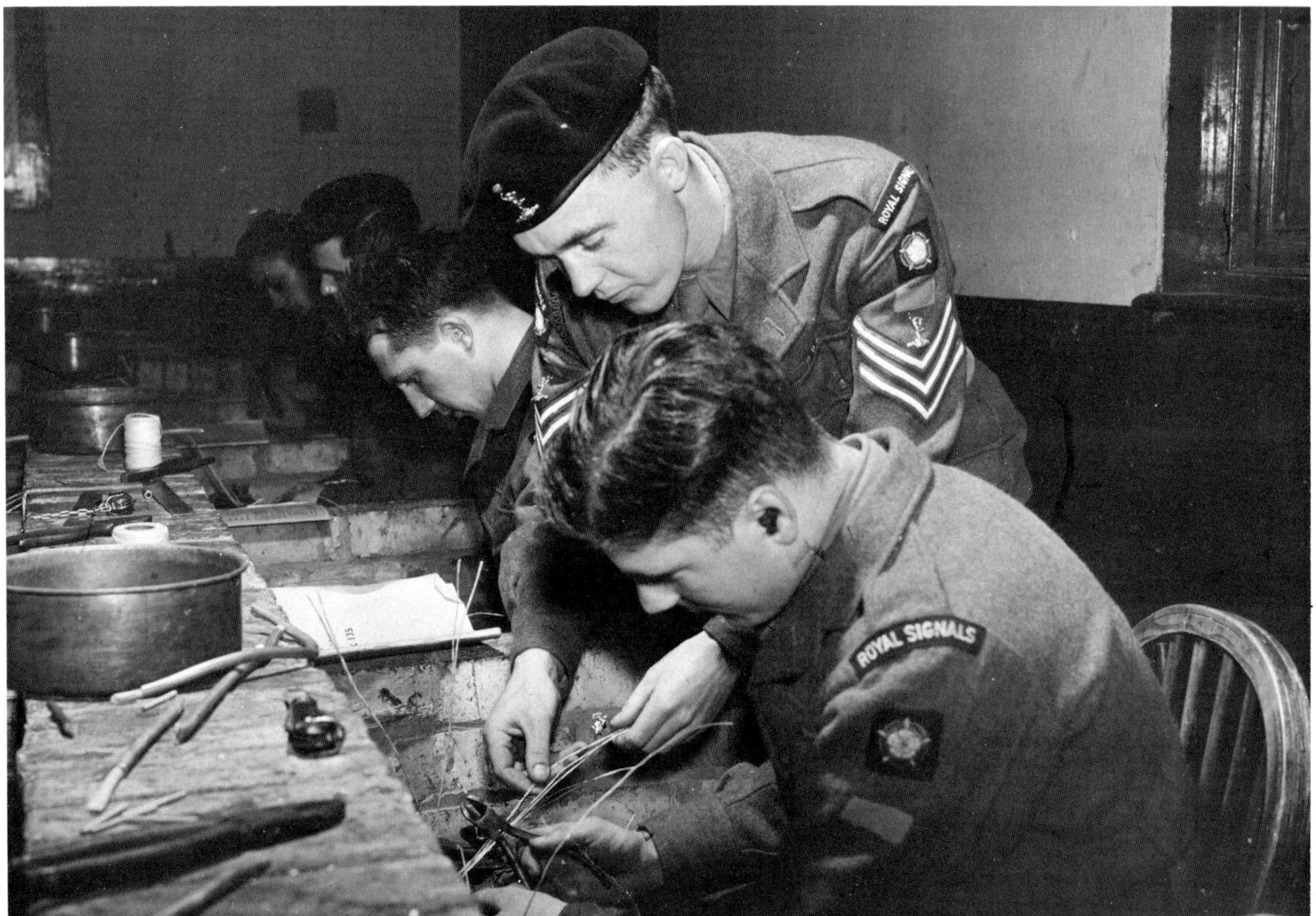
ROYAL SIGNALS

Left: Men of the RE Training Brigade carrying out bridging operations at Hawley Lake, Hants. *IWM*

Bottom left: Sgt Bailey, Line Mechanic, at the Royal Signals Training Establishment, Catterick Camp, instructs trainees on how to join multi-cables. *IWM*

Right: Signallers at work in a battalion command post during a training scheme. *IWM*

Below: A typical demonstration room of the MT Company, 1st Training Battalion, RASC, with the instructor explaining the mysteries of the internal combustion engine. *RCT Museum*

Bottom: Embryo RAMC medical orderlies learn all about the intricacies of sterilisation. *RAMC Historical Museum*

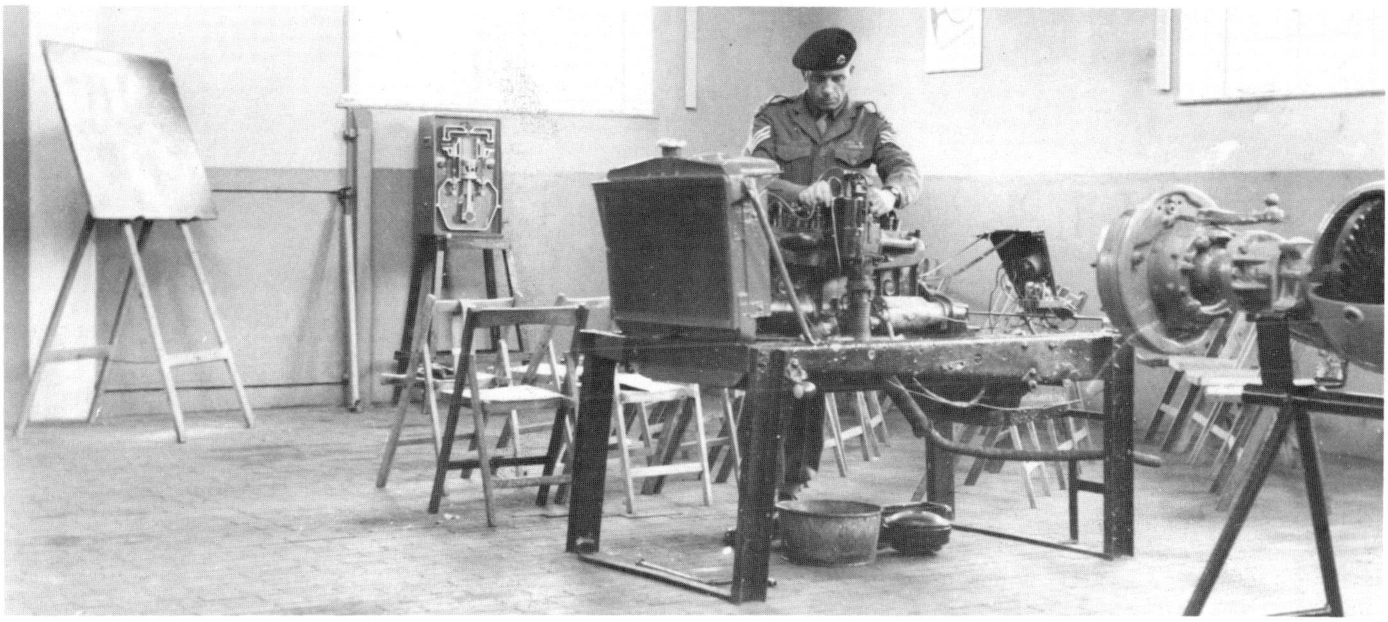

Above and right: All soldiers, especially the infantry, had to spend time on the open range, firing their personal weapons. These two photos show just how powerful is the soldier's best friend — the firing point is in Colchester and the butts in Cyprus! *IWM*

Below: Any pastrycook worth his salt would be proud of this magnificent creation. A young ACC recruit practices gateau decoration. *IWM*

Passing out

After trade training had been successfully completed, the 'fledglings' were ready to spread their wings and leave the nest to join units all over the world. But before they left their training regiments there was normally a really 'Bulled Up' passing out parade, sometimes attended by proud mums and dads, a platoon photo and much drinking!

Above left: DST takes the 'General Salute' at the Depot Battalion, RASC Bordon, July 1954. *RCT Museum*

Centre left: After the general salute came the inspection. *RCT Museum*

Below: And then the march past. *RCT Museum*

Top: 906 Recruit pass out at Southwood Camp, Cove, June 1954 (120 strong). Peter Fleur de Pledge who sent me this photo said that he was then a 'horrible sergeant' at Cove, and that they had only 16 weeks to turn recruits into Field Engineers B3 before their postings to service units. He closed his letter with the words: 'I have nothing but admiration for all the NS soldiers that I had contact with.' *Maj P. Fleur de Pledge*

Left: Alma and Somme platoons (NS intake) marching on to the pass out parade at Maindy Barracks, Cardiff, April 1952.
Welch Regiment Museum

Above: Squad photo of 81 Battery, 31 Training Regiment, RA, Kinmel Park. *RA Institution*

Top right: Squad photo of NS intake at Budbrooke Barracks, The Royal Warwickshire Regimental Depot, December 1955. From there they went out to join the battalion in Cyprus, sailing from Liverpool on 7 January 1956. *E. I. Hatton*

Centre right: Ex-Sgt Reg Rimmer, seen here with one of his pass out squads at the RPC Training Centre, Wrexham, said that his NS men were: 'generally well behaved . . . ' *R. Rimmer*

Below right: Mums and Dads attended pass out parades at the 64th Training Regiment, RA at Oswestry, so that they could see their sons on parade — they even sampled the food afterwards. *RA Institution*

Top: Pass out parades over and it was time to think about where they were going to serve. Here RASC drivers take their documents to the Depot Battalion office for check over. No doubt they were hoping to get to the 'Enchanted Isle' of Cyprus. *RCT Museum*

Right: The first leg of their journey was normally in the back of a three-tonner from the depot to the nearest railway station and then on to the troopship waiting for them at some port. *RCT Museum*

Below: 'It's special train for Atkins' when the trooper's on the tide!' A draft of the Royal Scots Greys gets ready to leave Catterick. The young officer on the right is of course HRH The Duke of Kent.
Sandes Soldiers' Homes

When the trooper's on the tide

In 1945 Britain's Troopship fleet numbered nearly 200 craft, but only three years later this number had been drastically reduced to 22 ships. By 1957 numbers were down to 14, although two new troopships (the *Nevasa* and the *Oxfordshire*) had been built and added to the fleet. Other famous ships were the *Asturias* (biggest and fastest), *Empire Fowey* and *Empire Orwell* (both former German vessels) and the chartered *Dilwara, Dunera* and *Devonshire*, all used on the Far East run. The ships on the Middle East run were the *Empire Ken*, the *Empire Clyde* and the *Cheshire*. In the late 1950s, the troopers carried 42,000 out of the 110,000 servicemen in transit each year. By 1960, there were only five troopships operating and by the time the last National Servicemen were leaving the Army, they had been completely replaced by air travel. There was something magical about the long journey out to the Far East in a troopship that air travel can never quite match, and those who were fortunate enough to experience it will never forget their time aboard a trooper.

Above left: Three lads from Yorkshire enjoying the view across the Bay of Biscay, on board the troopship *Oxfordshire*, bound for Hong Kong, June 1960. *IWM*

Below left: The *Empire Fowey*. Built in Hamburg in 1935, this fine old trooper began its days as the Nord Deutscher Lloyd liner the *Potsdam*. She was taken over as a war prize in 1945 and renamed, made one voyage to Port Said and then underwent an extensive five-year refit to bring her up to postwar trooping standards. Between 1950 and 1960, she carried over 40,000 Servicemen and their families across the seas. She was first used to take troops out to Korea in October 1950 and during the next four years made seven more trips to Korea. Her last military voyage was bringing home soldiers and their families from Cyprus in 1960, when she still managed to average 19kts. *Soldier*

Above: Leaving the *Oxfordshire* are men of the Queen's Royal Irish Hussars, who replaced the Royal Dragoons in Malaya in 1962.

Right: A young soldier gets a free copy of *Home News* as he disembarks in the Middle East. *Soldier*

Below: Sometimes Royal Naval vessels were used to move troops instead of troopships. Here men of the KOYLIs move on board the aircraft carrier HMS *Albion* in Singapore harbour on their way to relieve the Queen's Own Highlanders in Brunei. They are watched from the top deck by a Gurkha battalion who were also on their way to Brunei.

Goodnight Vienna!

Of course not all troopships were used on long runs. Smaller vessels, like the 4,326ton ss *Vienna*, carried a million and a half servicemen and their families between Harwich and the Hook of Holland, on their way to serve with the British Army of the Rhine. Even when air-trooping was introduced to BAOR in October 1950 and it was decided to dispense with the *Vienna*, her sister ships the *Empire Wansbeck* and *Empire Parkeston* still carried on, although their days too were sadly numbered.

Above left: Troops leaving the BAOR train at the Hook, to get on board their troopship to 'Blighty'. The 'Green', 'Red' and 'Blue' trains ran from the Hook to various parts of Germany. To start with there were no meal facilities on the trains and passengers had to get off at the border and eat at the station before going on with their journey. Later the Movements Branch of Northern Army Group hired dining cars from the German Dining Car Company, before specially designed and built rolling stock was brought into operation. Between them the three trains had seats for 1,128 passengers and the dining cars served over half a million lunches and the same number of teas each year. The trains also had travelling post offices used by the Army Post Office for Servicemen's mail. *Soldier*

Above: ss *Vienna*, her foremast dressed in farewell, lies alongside the Hook, while her soldier passengers make their way from the train. *Soldier*

Left: Once on board and settled in (remember those cramped, noisy berths in the bowels of the ship near the engine room?) it was time for life-belt drill. Here Troop Officer W. B. Causer, checks to ensure the tapes are properly tied. *Soldier*

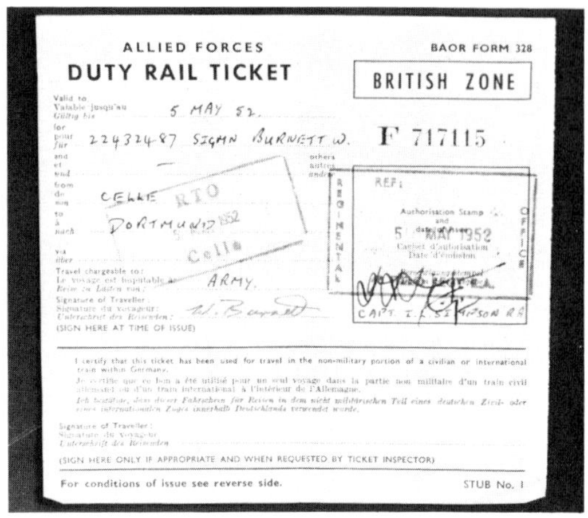

ALLIED FORCES

BAOR FORM 328

DUTY RAIL TICKET

BRITISH ZONE

Valid to / Valable jusqu'au / Gültig bis: 5 MAY 52.

for / pour / für: 22432487 SIGMN BURNETT W.

F 717115

and / et / und — others / autres / andere

from / de / von: CELLE

to / à / nach: DORTMUND

via / über

RTO 1952 Celle

Travel chargeable to: / Le voyage est imputable à / Reise zu Lasten von: ARMY.

Signature of Traveller: / Signature du voyageur: / Unterschrift des Reisenden: W. Burnett

(SIGN HERE AT TIME OF ISSUE)

REF:

REGIMENTAL — OFFICE

Authorisation Stamp and date of issue

5 MAY 1952

Cachet d'autorisation / Date d'émission

CAPT. I. L. SIMPSON RA

I certify that this ticket has been used for travel in the non-military portion of a civilian or international train within Germany.

Je certifie que ce bon a été utilisé pour un seul voyage dans la partie non militaire d'un train civil allemand ou d'un train international à l'intérieur de l'Allemagne.

Ich bestätige, dass dieser Fahrschein für Reisen in dem nicht militärischen Teil eines deutschen Zivil- oder eines internationalen Zuges innerhalb Deutschlands verwendet wurde.

Signature of Traveller: / Signature du voyageur / Unterschrift des Reisenden

(SIGN HERE ONLY IF APPROPRIATE AND WHEN REQUESTED BY TICKET INSPECTOR)

For conditions of issue see reverse side.

STUB No. 1

Top: All conditions on board were a bit cramped, but that didn't matter as it was a fairly short voyage. Here is the troop's canteen, with plenty of customers — so clearly it was a smooth crossing! *Soldier*

Left: Disembarking soldiers hand in pillow slips to RSM Bell, ex-Drum Major of the Royal Scots Fusiliers, who was the Ship's RSM. There was also of course a Ship's Commandant (Maj E. W. Young RPC). *Soldier*

Above: This duty rail ticket will probably stir a few memories of train journeys in BAOR. *Adam Forty*

Time to spare? Then go by air!

The gradual demise of the troopship meant that more and more servicemen and their families travelled by air, both on the short hop to Germany, and the longer flights to the Middle and Far East. The former was first instituted in late 1960, by Silver City Airways, flying *Hermes* aircraft from Manston, Kent, to Dusseldorf. Instead of a long and tiring 18-hour journey by train and troopship, there was a comfortable (?) 90-minute flight, with 'duty free beer and cigarettes and attractive hostesses'. To start with about 3,500 passengers were carried to Dusseldorf and Wildenrath each month and by the following autumn they had just about taken over the movement of the entire 200,000 yearly passengers to BAOR. A new air trooping centre was built opposite the civilian air terminal at Dusseldorf and the service steadily improved over the years.

Of course, as I have already said, some of the romance and excitement was lost when the relatively brief air flights replaced the month long sea voyage to the Far East. However, the early long distance flights were not without their own share of thrills. The trip took four days and there were no fewer than seven stops en route. At Rome, Nicosia, Bahrein, Karachi, Delhi, Calcutta and Bangkok, weary 'saddle-sore' passengers got off to stretch their legs, eat meals and spend two nights (or parts of them) actually sleeping in real beds — this was considered mandatory by the War Office, with the well being of the crew in mind as well as the comfort of the passengers. Civilian clothes had to be worn by all, so troops without were issued with 'suits civilian tropical grey' at the London Assembly Centre in Tottenham Court Road, and handed them in again on arrival in Singapore! In mid-1956, 20 Hermes IVA aircraft belonging to Airwork Ltd were used on the run, carrying 65 passengers (instead of the normal 68 so as to allow a little more legroom) in rear facing seats, with their 'Boots WD' safely tucked up on the racks with the cabin baggage — they were the only item of uniform which was worn.

Below left: Troops arriving at the Silver City Airways passenger terminal at Manston, November 1960. Uniform was allowed on the short BAOR flight, although in later years this was altered and civilian clothes were mandatory on all flights. *Soldier*

Below: Soldiers 'in disguise' as civilians wait to hand in their baggage at the departure terminal en route for Singapore in 1960. Civvies were worn so as not to alarm or annoy the authorities of the various airports at which the plane had to stop on the way to the Far East. *Soldier*

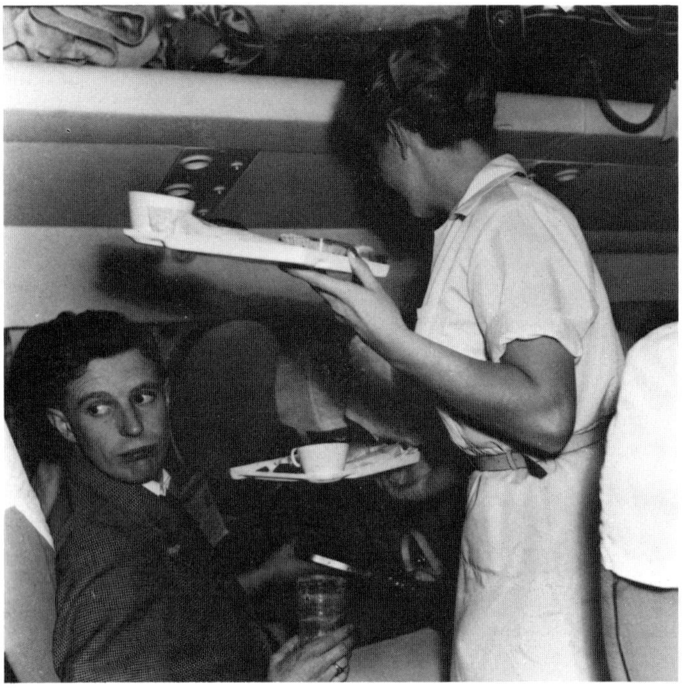

Above left: By 1960, the Hermes had been replaced by the Britannia, still run by Airwork Ltd of London. Here, the passengers join their aircraft on the tarmac. *Soldier*

Above right: 'Gentlemen you may smoke and unfasten your seat belts.' *Soldier*

Left: 'Just put it down there love, whilst I finish my pint.' *Soldier*

Aircraft of RAF Transport Command were also used to move troops and the photos show such a move to Gibraltar in March 1948. By the early 1960s the RAF were flying Comets on the Middle and Far East run, one of the refuelling places being the tiny tropical island of Gan in the Indian Ocean.

Below left: The platoon commander and platoon sergeant check flight details with skipper of the aircraft — an Avro York. *Soldier*

Below: 'Pick up your parrots and monkies and fall in facing the boat!' The draft, complete with FSMO, gets ready to load on to the aircraft. *Soldier*

Above: Confrontation between Malaysia and Indonesia. On 8 December 1962, the leader of the Brunei's People's Party launched a revolt, with forces trained in Indonesia. His aim was to unite Brunei, Sarawak and Sabah (all British territories) and join them with Indonesian Borneo. The rebels seized the oil town of Seria, but swift action by British and Gurkha troops ended the rebellion by 16 December. Here, men of the Queen's Own Highlanders load stores into an RAF Beverley on their way back to Singapore.
PR GHQ FARELF

Left: Soldiers of 1 Battalion, Devon and Dorset Regiment, emplaning into a Wessex helicopter of HMS *Devonshire* Ship's Flight. The flight disembarked in British Guiana.

With units

It is quite impossible in this short book to cover all aspects of life in units, so this chapter and the next one, which deals with the sort of jobs National Servicemen did in units, provide just a pot pourri of glimpses at regimental life — some ordinary, some bizarre, but all never to be forgotten by those who experienced them.

Right: Briefing for new arrivals on the 'delights' of Singapore by Sgt R. Johnson, South Wales Borderers, September 1957. *IWM*

Below right: Morning sick parade at Tampoi Camp, Malaya, December 1957. *IWM*

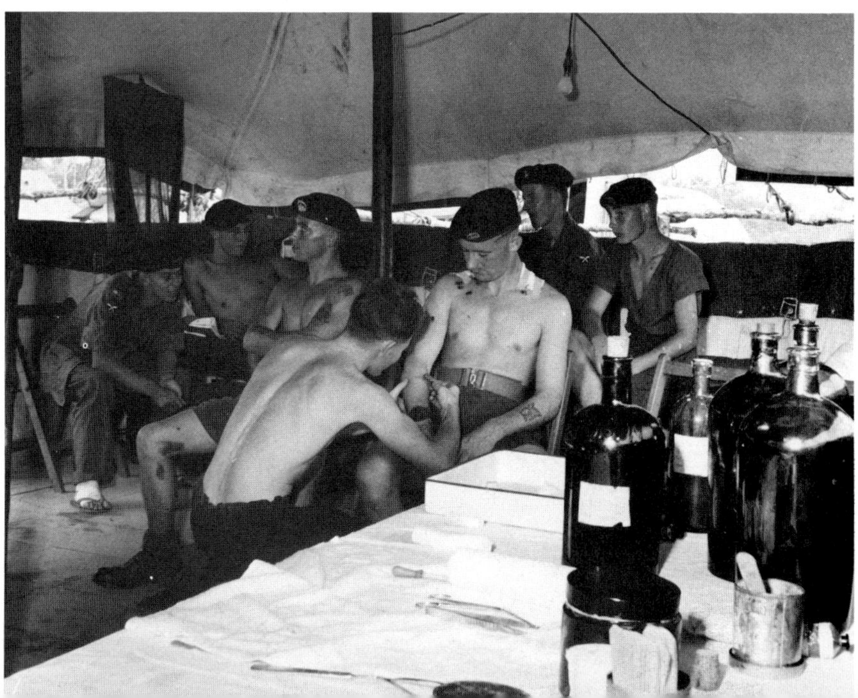

Left: 'Fits you like a glove!' New arrivals at Selerang Barracks, Singapore draw their jungle green uniforms. *IWM*

Below: 'Pay correct, Sir!' Men of the South Wales Borderers draw their pay at Tampoi Camp, Malaya, December 1957. *IWM*

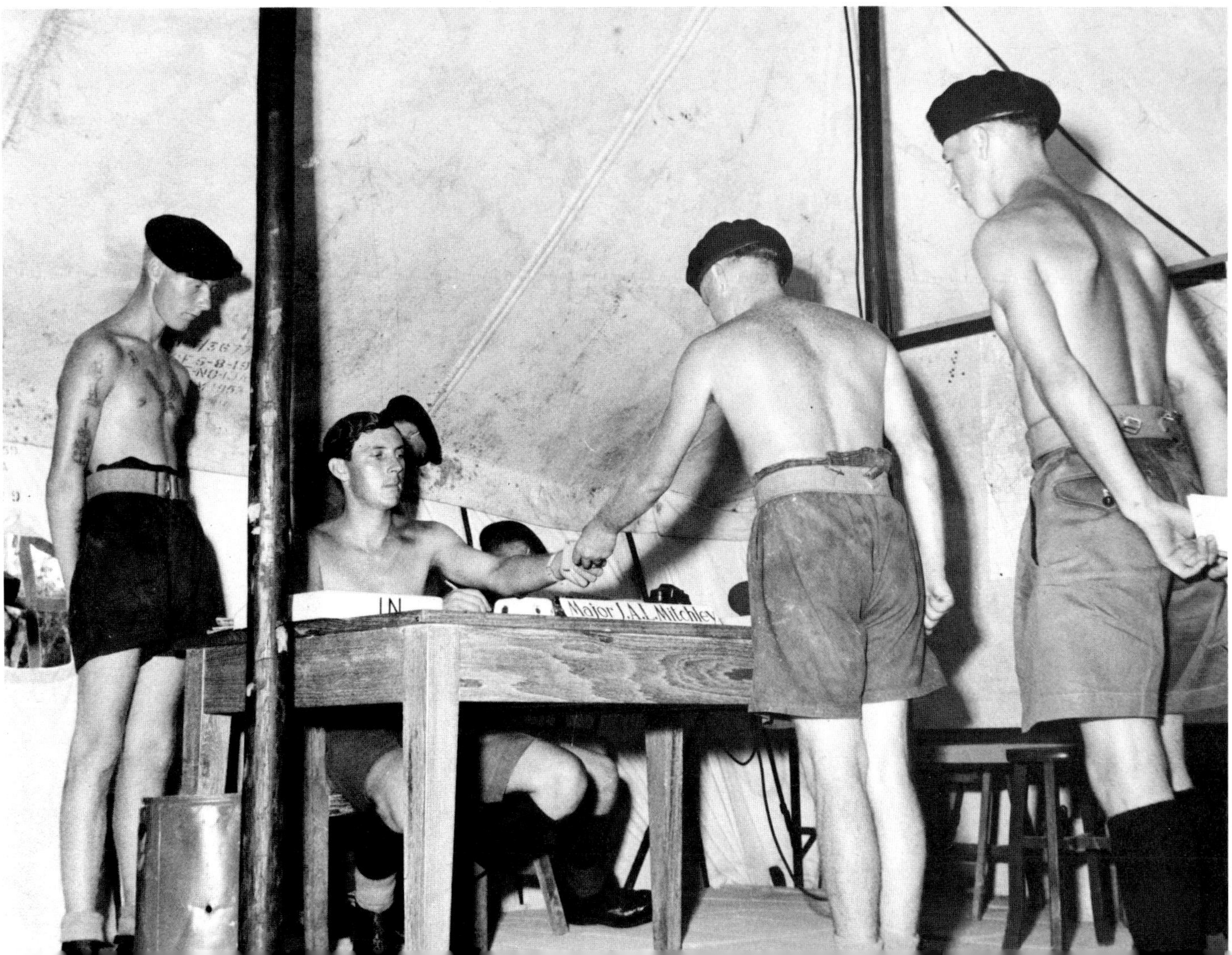

Above: This improvised shower was set up in a disused building in Nicosia. *Soldier*

Above right: Another makeshift shower, this one was in the Malayan jungle and was made out of old pieces of piping. *Alan Ward*

Centre right: Guardsmen always wear their splendid hats even when in tropical gear. This quartet was photographed at Beua Camp, in the British Cameroons in 1961. *R. G. White*

Below right: Tank crews on parade at the Queen's Bays tank park, Sabratha Barracks in Libya, May 1957. *IWM*

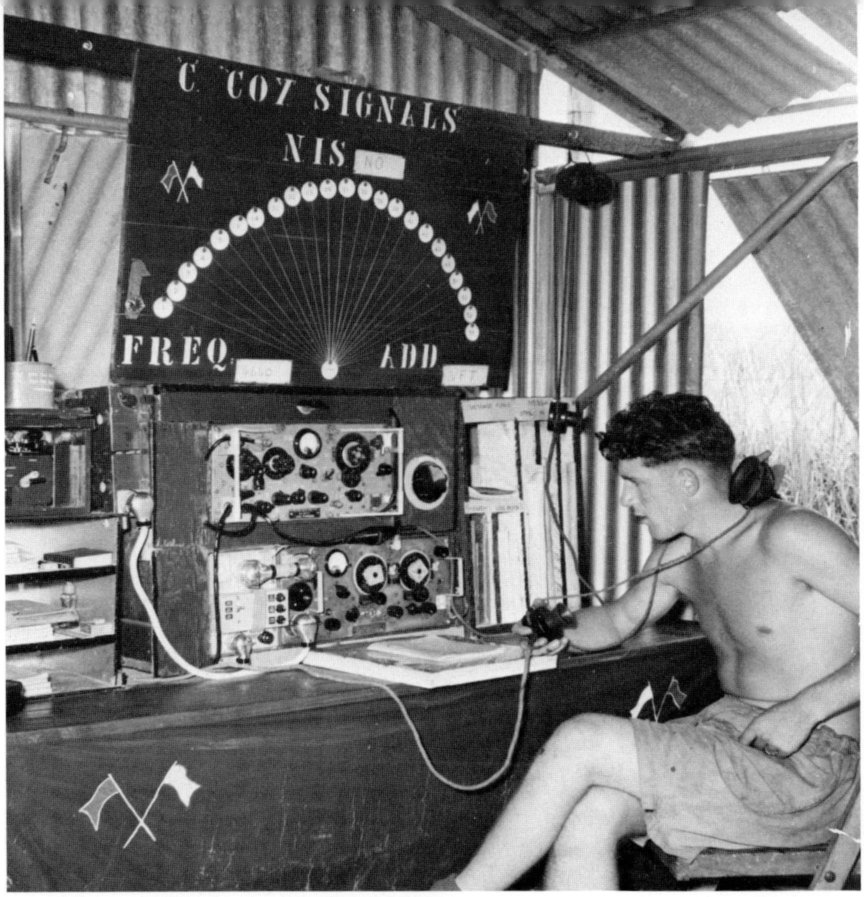

Above left: An operator keeps in touch with jungle patrols of C Company The King's Own Scottish Borderers, Yong Peng, Malaya, December 1957. *IWM*

Centre left: Divine Service attended by a handful of Green Jackets in a makeshift chapel in a village somewhere in Brunei.

Below: One of the advantages of teaching in the tropics is that you can always hold your classes outdoors. A 'schoolie' of 70 AEC, Singapore at work.

Left: Teaching Alsatian guard dogs to attack intruders was not much fun, even in a special suit and mask. *R. Wingham*

Above: Unless you happened to be in the RMP, this was one place you didn't ever want to be — inside an RMP incident room in Berlin. *Soldier*

Below left: Border patrols in the Hartz Mountains, West Germany made a pleasant change for Pat Rafferty and his Bren gun, March 1951. *P. J. Rafferty*

Below: 'Open wide, this won't hurt at all!' Dental surgery at the BMH Gibraltar, June 1960. *IWM*

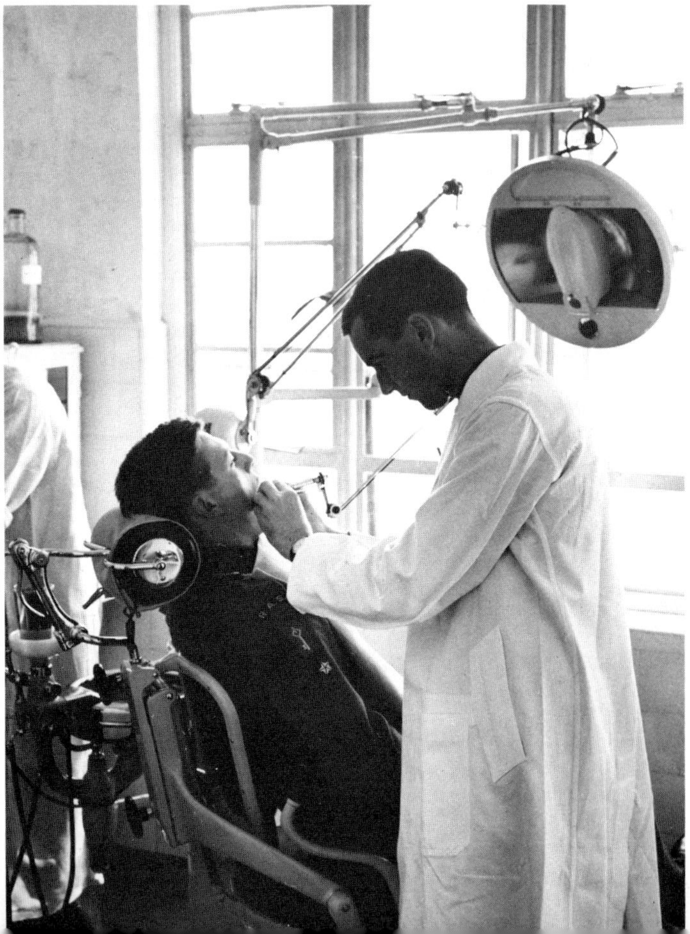

Top: Putting up tents in Germany during the exercise 'season'. *R. J. Spurway*

Above left: A very odd type of training for RMP dog handlers in Cyprus involved swimming in full kit (minus dogs!). *R. Wingham*

Above: Practising his fast draw is Ron Wingham of the RMP dog handlers in Cyprus. *R. Wingham*

Left: When there was no grass to cut or stones to paint then the sand had to be 'bulled'! If I hadn't seen it I would never have believed it. *J. Mann*

Above: No guesses on what they are digging, I just hope no one fell in! *J. Mann*

Above right and right: Local newspapers from home always provided a welcome change no matter where one was serving: John Mann and Roy Kitchenman in Fayid ; a group of Gordon Highlanders in Cyprus.
J. Mann, PR Cyprus

Below right: One of the many 'shrines' to the great god 'Bullshit', where his slaves spent many happy hours polishing such sacred objects as pickhelves, spades and steel helmets — to be used at your peril or they might get dirty! This 'shrine' was the troop stores of the Royal Signals troop attached to 43 Field Regiment, RA, so they did have to use the contents, except when it was prepared for the annual administration inspection.
W. Burnett

The jobs they did

The variety of jobs undertaken by NS men were legion — here are but a small selection and I apologise in advance to all those I have missed out.

Left: The Sovereign's Escort of the Household Cavalry leaving Hyde Park Barracks for the State Opening of Parliament. *IWM*

Below: The crew of a Centurion tank belonging to the Queen's Bays stop for a 'brew' during training in the Libyan desert, May 1957. *IWM*

Above: Saladins and Ferrets exercise in the desert near Benghazi.

Centre left: A very smart gun crew of National Servicemen man their 25-pounder. *Soldier*

Below left: A quartet of gunner regimental buglers. *RA Institution*

Above right: The gun crew of a 3.7in anti-aircraft gun belonging to 37HAA Regiment, RA, goes into action during firing practice in Malta, May 1957. *IWM*

Above far right: A sapper makes short work of a gum tree in Kenya. The trees were used to repair a culvert that had been damaged during floods in October 1961.

Below right: A field detachment of No 89 Field Survey Squadron, RE, carry out a survey expedition near Garissa, Kenya, March-April 1959. *PR Army*

Left: J. R. Humphreys, photographed here in his scarlet uniform, did public duties in London as well as serving in the Malayan jungles in 1948-9. *J. R. Humphreys*

Above: Men of the PWO training on the Mobat anti-tank gun at Buenovista Baracks, Gibraltar, June 1960. *IWM*

Below: With blackened faces, men of the DERR follow up the initial assault in Mellieha Bay, Malta, during an exercise. *IWM*

Above left: South Wales Borderers MT Section pose for a photo in the vehicle park at Selerang Barracks, Singapore, September 1957. *IWM*

Top: A Signals despatch rider belonging to the Signals Troop, attached to 43 Field Regiment, RA, at Dortmund. *W. Burnett*

Above: Radio operator Walter Burnett, mans his Wireless No 19 in the back of a 15cwt truck. *W. Burnett*

Left: RASC DUKWs leaving the water during Exercise 'Soft Line'. The DUKW was but one of the many vehicles which the RASC had to learn how to drive. *RCT Museum*

R.A.M.C

Vanguard

Far left: This RAMC medical assistant had a floating sickbay on board a troopship for his National Service. *Soldier*

Left: Driving a staff car was not really a 'cushy number' and involved long hours and plenty of 'bull', especially for drivers in London, like this 1956 vintage Standard Vanguard driver, who worked for the War Office. *RCT Museum*

Below left: Four RAMC stretcher bearers carry a casualty up a steep rocky path amid the 'Barren Rocks of Aden' — part of the Little Aden oil refinery can be seen in the background.

Right: Men of 'C' Air Supply Platoon of the RASC Air Despatch at Nicosia training in handling and loading of heavy equipment on to aircraft.

Centre right: Two men of 55 Company, RASC, load supplies for parachuting to the 3rd Battalion of the Malay Regiment during jungle operations, November 1957. *IWM*

Bottom right: Vehicle Mechanics lower a new Meteor engine into a Centurion tank. *IWM*

Above: The bright lights of Berlin were the 'home town beat' for these RMPs. *Soldier*

Right: L Cpl Ron Wingham with his beautiful Alsatian 'Wonder War Dog' called *Prest*. Cyprus 1959. *R. Wingham*

Below: Regimental Policemen of 22 LAA Regiment, RA, at Menden BAOR, 1949. *T. Coleman*

Above left: Typing company orders in a luxuriously appointed office in 1st Battalion Grenadier Guards in the British Cameroons. *R. G. White*

Centre left: PTIs display their prowess. *RA Institution*

Below: The cookhouse staff of the Royal Welch Fusiliers in Germany. *E. J. Spurway*

Above: Mess waiters, barman and batmen were all indispensable jobs in any unit, but were probably among the least popular pursuits for National Servicemen. *IWM*

Right: The Regimental Band rehearses. *IWM*

Below: 'Not a bad chap' was the caption to this photograph of a young platoon officer of the Leicesters, who commanded 'Nancy's Knockabouts'. *A. Ward*

Commissioned

Whilst at their Training Regiments certain NS men were earmarked for training as officers. The first major step was to attend a War Office Selection Board (WOSB) where potential officers (known as 'POs') were put through a series of tests designed to see if they had the right qualities of leadership, initiative etc. I remember a friend of mine, when at his WOSB, was mad keen to show the DS (Directing Staff) what an excellent footballer he was and leapt in the air to head away the ball which one of the DS tossed from a first storey verandah to the POs waiting expectantly below. Unfortunately the ball was full of wet sand and so he went out like a light! Nevertheless he passed the WOSB which shows you can't keep a good man down!

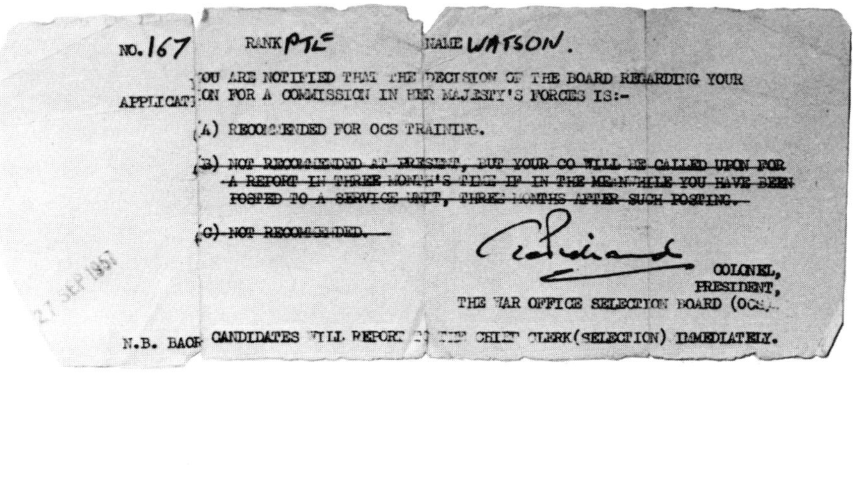

NO. 167 RANK PTE NAME WATSON.

YOU ARE NOTIFIED THAT THE DECISION OF THE BOARD REGARDING YOUR APPLICATION FOR A COMMISSION IN HER MAJESTY'S FORCES IS:-

(A) RECOMMENDED FOR OCS TRAINING.

~~(B) NOT RECOMMENDED AT PRESENT, BUT YOUR CO WILL BE CALLED UPON FOR A REPORT IN THREE MONTH'S TIME IF IN THE MEANWHILE YOU HAVE BEEN POSTED TO A SERVICE UNIT, THREE MONTHS AFTER SUCH POSTING.~~

~~(C) NOT RECOMMENDED.~~

COLONEL,
PRESIDENT,
THE WAR OFFICE SELECTION BOARD (OCS)

21 SEP 1957

N.B. BACK CANDIDATES WILL REPORT TO THE CHIEF CLERK(SELECTION) IMMEDIATELY.

Above: A squad of smiling NS men at their WOSB — clearly this was taken *before* and not after the tests were completed. *Rev D. C. Hodgson*

Left: Just a little scrap of paper but it meant so much! *Adam Forty*

And then it was off to OCTU! NS officers were trained at two main Officer Cadet Schools, *Eaton Hall* for infantry (including the Brigade of Guards), REME, RMP, Intelligence Corps, RAMC, RAOC and RAEC (basic officer training only for the last three); the remainder went to *Mons*. The photos which follow illustrate the work at one of these two illustrious and now defunct establishments, and appeared in an article in *Soldier* magazine entitled 'The Eatonians'. Here officer cadets spent 16 weeks, divided into two phases. The first six weeks was basic military training, after which RAMC, RAOC and REME cadets went off to their own special arms schools. The rest stayed for a further 10 weeks' infantry training. All this training was carried out amid the Victorian splendour of the Duke of Westminster's mansion and 350-acre estate, which he had leased to the War Office in 1947.

Right: Cadets march through the 200-year old 'Golden Gates' of Eaton Hall OCS, near Chester. *Soldier*

Above: The dulcet tones of RSM A. Tomlinson, Coldstream Guards echo around the drill square. *Soldier*

Above right: The 'Wounded Amazon' modestly turns her back, lest she distract the attention of the biliards players. *Soldier*

Right: Eaton Hall boasted one of the toughest assault courses in the Army. This chainwalk is suspended between trees 15ft off the ground. *Soldier*

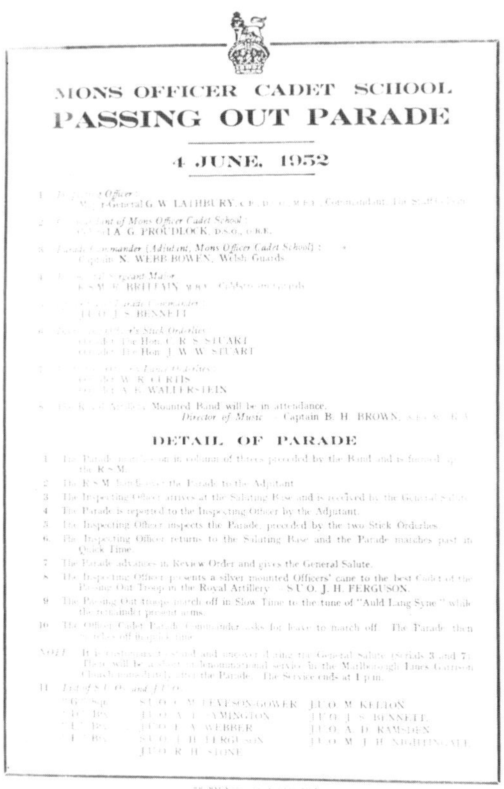

MONS OFFICER CADET SCHOOL

PASSING OUT PARADE

4 JUNE, 1952

1. Inspecting Officer:
Major-General G. W. LATHBURY, [illegible], Commandant, The Staff College
2. Commandant of Mons Officer Cadet School:
Colonel A. G. PROUDLOCK, D.S.O., O.B.E.
3. Parade Commander (Adjutant, Mons Officer Cadet School):
Captain N. WEBB-BOWEN, Welsh Guards.
4. Regimental Sergeant Major:
R.S.M. R. BRITTAIN, M.B.E., Coldstream Guards
5. [illegible] Parade Commander:
J.U.O. J. S. BENNETT
6. Inspecting Officer's Stick Orderlies:
O/Cadet The Hon. C. R. S. STUART
O/Cadet The Hon. J. W. W. STUART
7. [illegible] Orderlies:
O/Cdt. W. R. CURTIS
O/Cdt. A. E. WALLERSTEIN
8. The Royal Artillery Mounted Band will be in attendance.
Director of Music — Captain B. H. BROWN, [illegible]

DETAIL OF PARADE

1. The Parade marches on in column of threes preceded by the Band and is formed up by the R.S.M.
2. The R.S.M. hands over the Parade to the Adjutant.
3. The Inspecting Officer arrives at the Saluting Base and is received by the General Salute.
4. The Parade is reported to the Inspecting Officer by the Adjutant.
5. The Inspecting Officer inspects the Parade, preceded by the two Stick Orderlies.
6. The Inspecting Officer returns to the Saluting Base and the Parade marches past in Quick Time.
7. The Parade advances in Review Order and gives the General Salute.
8. The Inspecting Officer presents a silver mounted Officers' cane to the best Cadet of the Passing Out Troop in the Royal Artillery — S.U.O. J. H. FERGUSON.
9. The Passing Out troops march off in Slow Time to the tune of "Auld Lang Syne" while the remainder present arms.
10. The Officer Cadet Parade Commander asks for leave to march off. The Parade then marches off in quick time.

NOTE. It is customary to stand and uncover during the General Salute (Serials 3 and 7). There will be a short undenominational service in the Marlborough Lines Garrison Church immediately after the Parade. The Service ends at 1 p.m.

11. List of S.U.O's and J.U.O's:

[illegible]	S.U.O. C. M. LEVESON-GOWER	J.U.O. M. KELTON
[illegible]	J.U.O. A. [illegible] SYMINGTON	J.U.O. J. S. BENNETT
[illegible]	J.U.O. [illegible] A. WEBBER	J.U.O. A. D. RAMSDEN
[illegible]	S.U.O. J. H. FERGUSON	J.U.O. M. J. H. NIGHTINGALE
	J.U.O. R. H. STONE	

The greatest day in the life of each officer cadet was the day he passed out and received his National Service commission. The pictures that follow were taken on a variety of passing out parades, some of those at Mons OCS being instantly made recognisable by the unforgettable figure of RSM Ronald Brittain, MBE, probably the most well known RSM in the postwar British Army.

Left: Details of a Mons OCS Passing Out Parade for 4 June 1952. *Adam Forty*

Above: The Senior Under Officer (on left), JUO, Company Commander and Adjutant just before the Pass Out parade at Buller Barracks in September 1954 (RASC cadets did six weeks at Mons, then 10 weeks at Buller). On this particular parade the SUO stamped so hard when reporting the parade ready for inspection that his trouser legs escaped from his gaiters! *Lt-Col P. Love*

Right: 'General Salute, present arms!' *Lt-Col P. Love*

Above: Inspection of those passing out at Buller Barracks, September 1954. *Lt-Col P. Love*

Left: With the familiar figure of RSM Brittain close the saluting base, the inspecting officer takes the general salute at Mons OCS. *Soldier*

Bottom left: Maj-Gen Lathbury, Commandant of The Staff College, inspects the Mons OCS passing out parade, 4 June 1952. *P. Jackson*

Above right: Presenting the best cadet with a suitably inscribed swagger cane. ***Soldier***

Below right: Those being commissioned march off parade and up the steps whilst the remainder present arms. *P. Jackson*

Left: The adjutant on his horse follows the passing off squad up the steps. Pat Love told me that on at least one occasion, the horse was 'watered' with a bucket of mixed drinks the night before a pass out — a worried looking groom could be seen the following morning leading a very groggy horse around the square desperately trying to sober it up before parade. *Soldier*

Below: Marching off at Buller. *Lt-Col P. Love*

Bottom: Cadet Company 1 Training Brigade, RASC, 1954. *Lt-Col P. Love*

Training exercises

Generally speaking everyone, particularly those in the 'teeth' arms, liked getting out of barracks on training exercises, after all, it was more like being a real soldier and the 'bull' and all those seemingly unnecessary regulations and restrictions were relaxed. Salisbury Plain was the favourite battlefield in UK, whilst the autumn exercises in BAOR ranged far and wide all over the newly harvested fields of the North German plain.

Above: Those who served in the Royal Armoured Corps in Germany will long remember the tank train to Hohne. A familiar sight to all 'tankies' is this view of part of a squadron of Centurions on their way to Hohne for annual firing. All RAC regiments in BAOR took their AFVs to Hohne for a hectic fortnight of open range firing, the culmination of the year's gunnery training. *G. Forty*

Centre left: Tanks of 1 RTR pause beside the well known 'Windmill' landmark on the Sennelager Training Area, spring 1949. *G. Forty*

Below left: Armoured cars of the Life Guards take part in night operations during Exercise 'Autumn Flight' on Salisbury Plain in 1957. *Soldier*

Above: A West Yorks bazooka team get ready to engage advancing enemy tanks during Exercise 'Autumn Flight'. *Soldier*

Centre right: These men of the Royal Scots Fusiliers were flown in to RAF Odiham for Exercise 'Autumn Flight' by RAF Transport Command. Note the spectators near one of the range towers. *Soldier*

Below right: A well camouflaged Bofors gun gets ready to engage enemy aircraft. *Soldier*

Above: Highlight of Exercise 'Autumn Flight' was a night drop by men of 1 Parachute Battalion, with the aid of flares. They took the enemy by surprise during their daring night raid. *Soldier*

Centre left: A paratrooper shepherds his prisoners to the POW camp as Exercise 'Autumn Flight' draws to a close. *Soldier*

Below left: Briefing for a night patrol on the Thetford training area, December 1961. *IWM*

Above: 3in mortar detachments in action. *IWM*

Right: This fighting patrol has been taken close to enemy lines in an Army Air Corps helicopter. *IWM*

Below right: Infantrymen practise a night river crossing in rubber boats. *IWM*

The real thing

The real test of a soldier has got to be the way he acts in battle. National Servicemen were tested in the most bloody conditions all over the world and, as one might have expected, despite their irritation with and dislike for anything to do with military discipline, they proved themselves to be every bit as good as any other British soldier throughout history. Nearly 400 were killed in action in such places as Palestine, Korea, Malaya, the Canal Zone, Cyprus and Kenya. Their commanding officers wrote about their bravery in the most glowing terms and it is a pity that there is only sufficient space in this book to show but a few of these gallant young men in action.

Above: Two young soldiers of the Royal Sussex 'off duty' in their well protected Korean 'hutchie', c1951. *IWM*

Left: Young NS men of the Welch Regiment sing 'Sospan Fach' to harmonica accompaniment during a brief lull somewhere in Korea. *Welch Regiment Museum*

Left: Another patrol is briefed, Korea c1952. *IWM*

Below: A Troop of 48th Field Regiment in action against a terrorist hideout near Negri Sembilan, Malaya, December 1957. *IWM*

Above: Armoured cars in a night engagement with terrorists at Sungei Kluang near Ipoh, November 1957. *IWM*

Right: A new draft of the KOSB's receiving instruction in jungle warfare at Batu Bahat, December 1957. *IWM*

Below right: Men of No 2 Platoon, A Company, of the Cameronians, receive their ammunition and grenades from their platoon sergeant, prior to a jungle patrol, in Malaya.

TRADE MARK
12 PLN
NANCY'S
KNOCKABOUTS

Left: The dummy wears the uniform of Yong Hoi, self confessed killer of more than 100 people.

Below far left: Platoon sign in the Royal Leicesters camp in Malaya. *A. Ward*

Below left: An alert sentry of Leicesters stands guard on the perimeter of a jungle camp, somewhere in Malaya. *A. Ward*

Above right and centre right: Both show men of 13 Infantry Workshop on jungle training in 1961. *W. Ashby*

Below: Men of the Green Jackets going up river during anti terrorist operations in Brunei.

Above left: Ready to deal with a mob of rioters is this KOYLI squad pictured in Singapore.

Centre left: Practising riot squad drill, Kenya, February 1961. *PR Army*

Below: A young Bren gunner keeps watch from the battlements of Kyrenia Castle, Cyprus, May 1957. *IWM*

Right: Riot drill features regularly in unit training programmes in Cyprus, May 1957. *IWM*

Below right and bottom right: Two who paid the supreme sacrifice are buried with full military honours in Singapore on 22 October 1953. *Lt-Col A. J. Barker*

Get out of me bedspace!

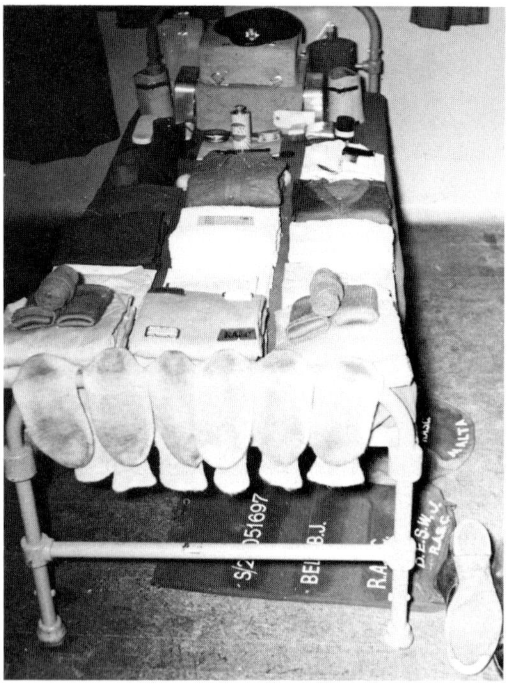

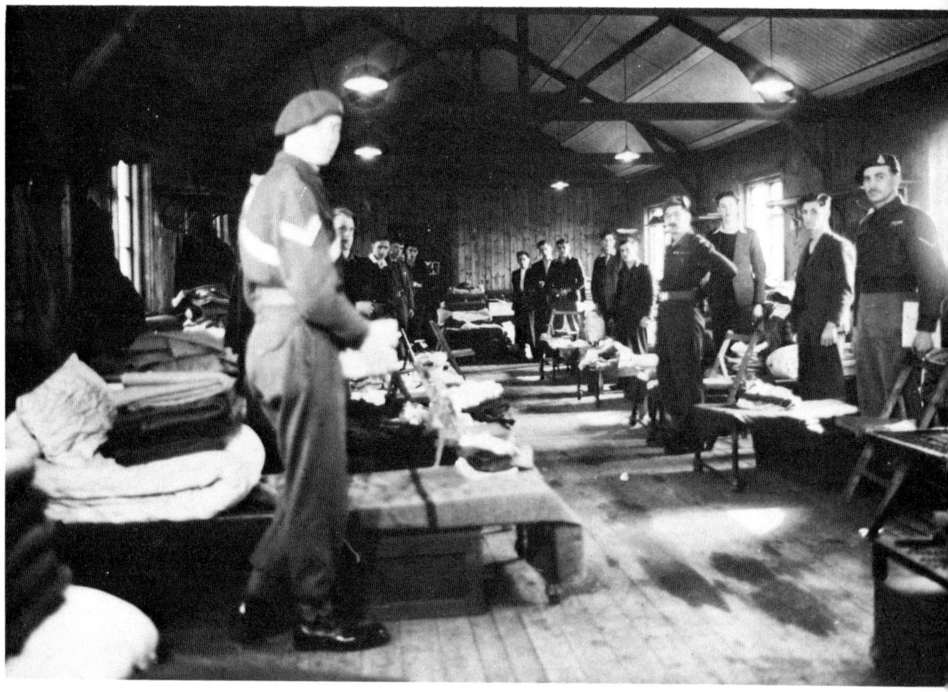

Could there be a more evocative catch-phrase than this one? It was a plea that every National Serviceman learned to invoke very early in his Army service. Nobody *ever* entered another's bedspace during training for fear of scratching the laboriously polished floor. And on nights before those barrack room inspections, after spending hours polishing everything one possessed, including the studs on the soles of one's boots, the backs as well as the front of one's brasses and capbadge, then you settled down to a night on the floor because there just wouldn't be time to lay out all your kit in the frantic few hours of daylight the next morning. Instead, that time was devoted to polishing the usually grotty and polish encrusted surface of the floor of the old wooden 'spider' type hut which was 'home' during training in UK. Thereafter, billets came in all shapes and sizes as the photos show, but you never ever completely forgot that very first bedspace.

Above right: The first batch of NS men received by 1st Training Battalion, RAOC in Aldershot, March 1948, were allocated these typical bedspaces in their 'spider'. *RAOC Museum*

Above: A sight to gladden the heart of any sergeant! A good kit layout at the RASC Training Brigade. *RCT Museum*

Right: With a shine like that on the floor this couldn't be anywhere but the Guards Depot. *Soldier*

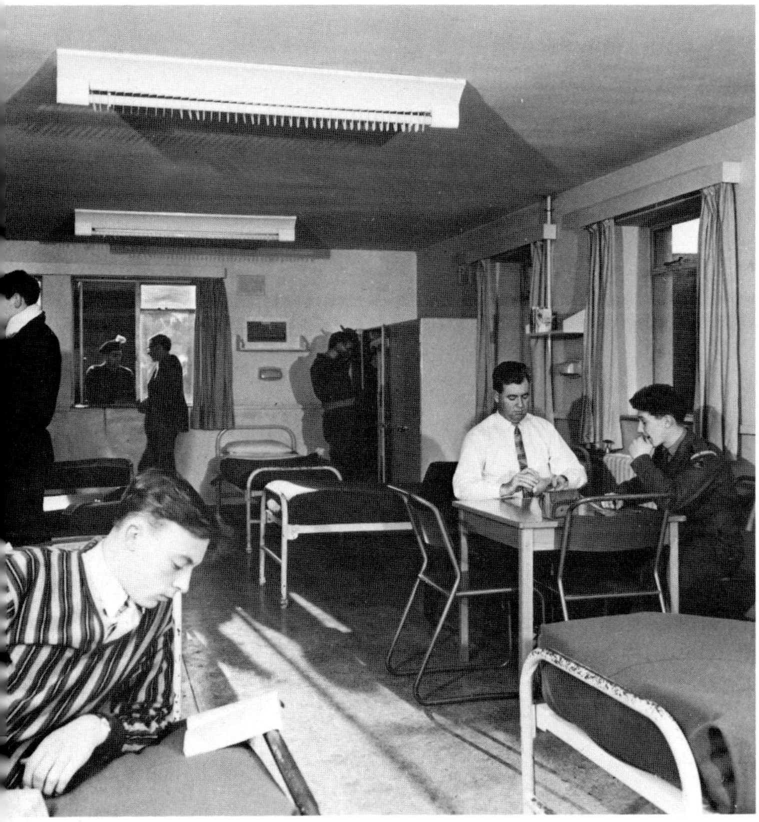

Above: The shape of things to come. A new barrack room at Hyderabad Barracks, Colchester, is still functional but a great improvement on the old wooden huts. December 1961. *IWM*

Right: High ceilings and plenty of fresh air in this Singapore barrack room. *IWM*

Below: The floors of these tents in Tampoi Camp, Malaya, were covered with stone slabs so that they were easier to keep clean in the wet season. *IWM.*

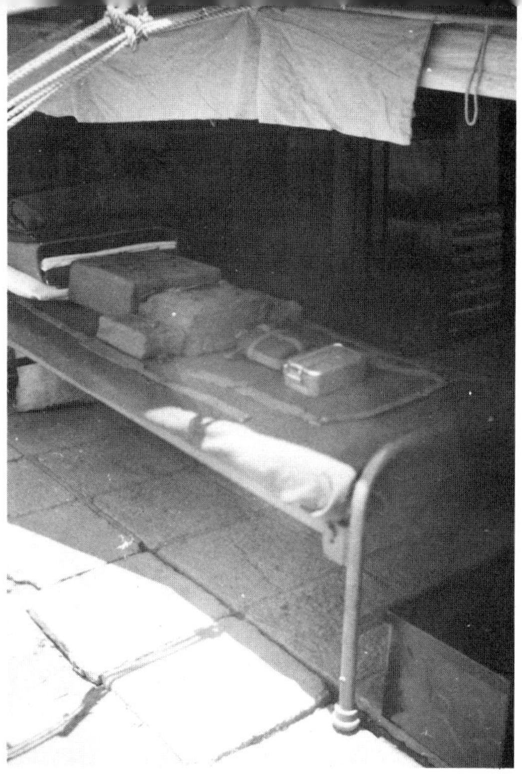

Above left: Most troops in Cyprus had to live in tents, both winter and summer, but the garrison of Kyrenia Castle were much better off. Their barrack rooms were set inside the immensely thick walls of the 12th century Crusaders' castle, so they were cool in summer and warm in winter. *IWM*

Top: This was John Mann's bedspace and kit layout for the annual Administration Inspection in the Canal Zone, 1955. *J. Mann*

Above: This smart locker layout in Keat Hong, Malaya, belonged to Cpl Royston Hale, RAOC, who served all over Malaya and Singapore 1954-56. One can readily see why Royston now works for Burton's Menswear in Sutton Coldfield! *R. J. Hale*

Left: Tropical bedspace with mosquito net and pinups. *W. Ashby*

Left: Some bedspaces were completely outdoors, like these 'pup tents' in the Malayan jungle.
Lt-Col A. J. Barker

Below and below left: Off with the old — on with the new! For years this was the normal Aldershot barrack room — cheerless and draughty, where the only comfort was to be found by huddling around a dirty and petulant stove (shades of Cinderella!) However, in the early 1960s Aldershot started to receive its share of a 'facelift' in which £50million was spent on new barracks all over UK between 1960 and 1966. Too late alas to improve the lot of most NS men. *Soldier*

Bottom: These strange looking huts were 'home' to Royal Signals trainees at Gallowgate Camp, Catterick. If one left the hut doors ajar during the winter months then the sheep came in off the moor!
W. Burnett

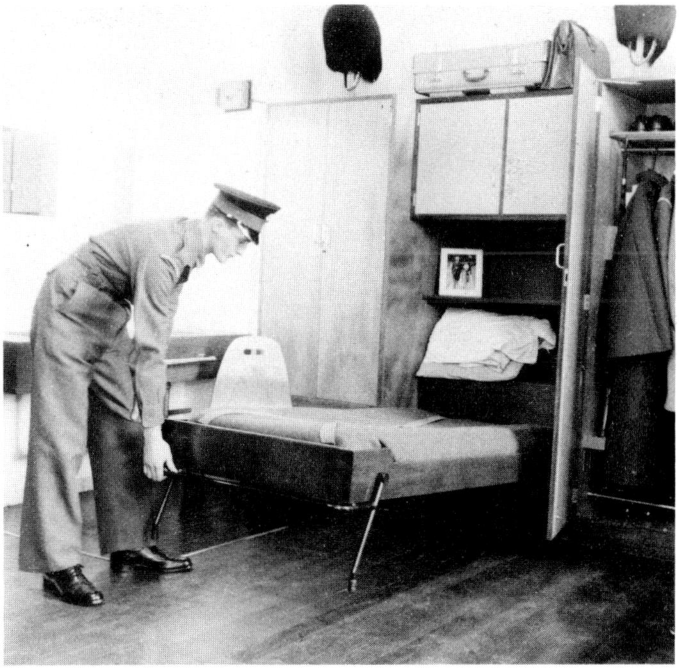

Food, glorious food!

Army food and army cooks have long been the object of rude jokes and ridicule, much of it completely unfounded. Certainly nowadays, Army food is of the very highest quality and is on the whole well cooked by well trained cooks. During the National Service era it was, like the curate's egg — 'good in parts'.

Right: 'Double, double, toil and trouble, fire burn and cauldron bubble'. What fiendish brew is 'cookie' concocting for us today? *IWM*

Below: Typical cookhouse scene, as luncheon is prepared at Hyderabad Barracks, Colchester. *IWM*

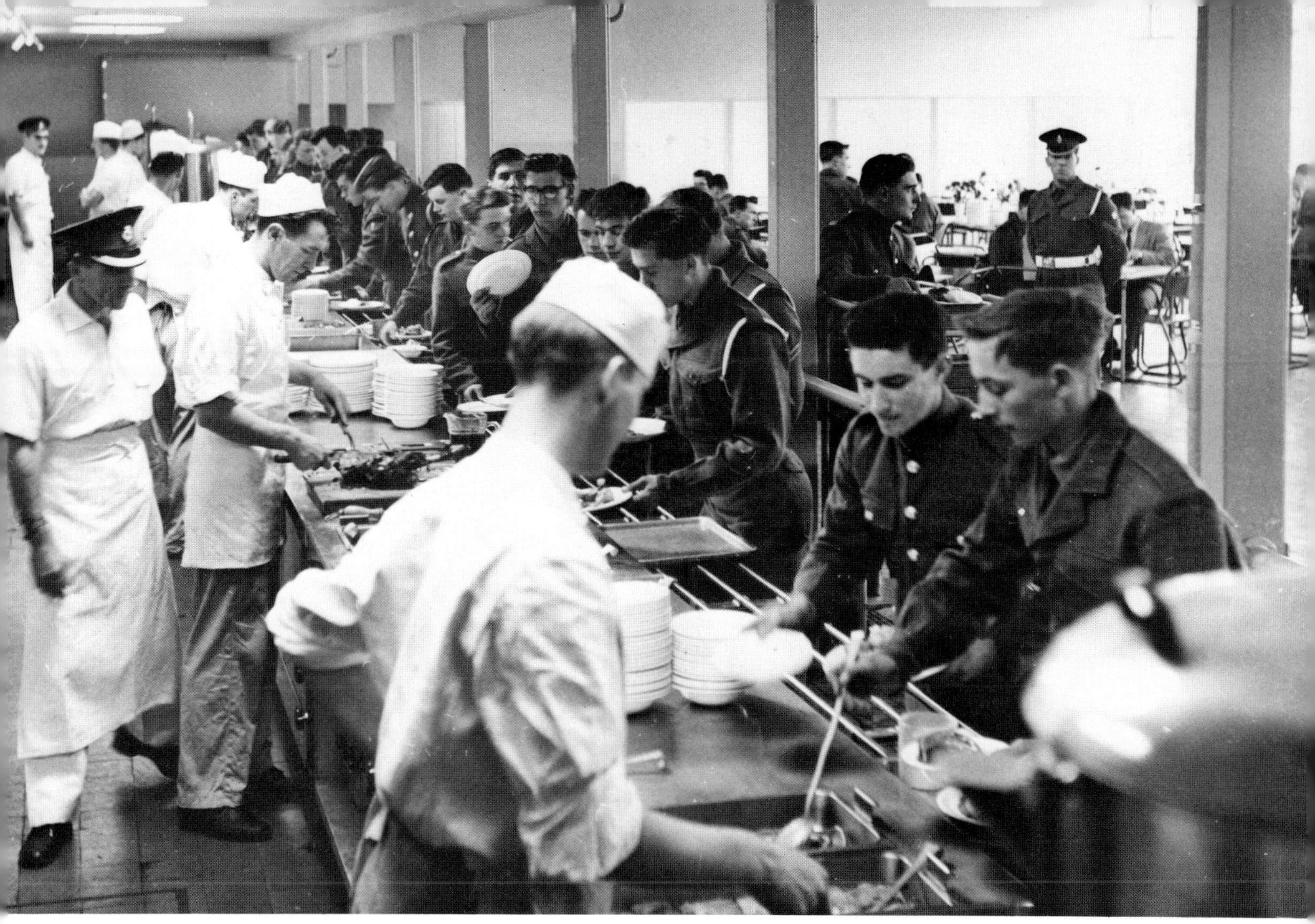

Above: It's 'help yourself' in this new cookhouse/restaurant at the Cavalry Barracks, Windsor. *IWM*

Left: The Rifle Brigade camp at Negri Sembilan, Malaya, in December 1957, was set on a hill so that the soldiers could receive the benefit of any breezes. Here riflemen eat their midday meal. *IWM*

Below left: Cookhouses in BAOR usually employed German labour as well as ACC cooks as this photo shows. I wonder why the cook corporal is eyeing the 'duff' with that worried expression? *E. J. Spurway*

Above: A party of jolly ACC cooks attached to the Royal Welch Fusiliers in Germany, chop up the morning veg during outdoor training exercises. *E. J. Spurway*

Left: In Malaya, rations came in by airdrop when patrols were operating deep in the jungle. *A. D. Barrowcliff*

Above right: This sort of magnificent spread was the work of the ACC cooks attached to 1 RWF at Christmas 1947. *E. J. Spurway*

Centre right: This Saturday morning cookhouse inspection was rather a special one, as Field Marshal Montgomery (not looking at all well) was the surprise visitor to the 1 RWF cookhouse. *E. J. Spurway*

Far right: Shades of 'Three Men in a Boat' and the tin of pineapple! Attempting the impossible with a machete during jungle training.

Below right: Men of the Loyal Regiment enjoy a snack in their jungle camp, during anti-terrorist operations in Perak State, November 1957. *IWM*

Faraway places with strange sounding names

National Service did provide a wonderful opportunity for visiting all sorts of faraway places. This was one of the major advantages of being an NS man, and one which many have written to me about, with a certain wistful longing for those exciting days. Certainly those who did have the good fortune to serve abroad were generally happier, better behaved and much better motivated, than those stuck in England. This chapter shows but a small selection of the exotic places soldiers visited.

Above left: Two troopers who are on their way to join the 10th Royal Hussars in Aqaba (Persian Gulf) abroad the troopship *Empire Ken*, stop off for few hours in Malta. They are seen haggling with the driver of a horse-drawn 'gharry' about the price of a sightseeing trip around Valetta, May 1957. *IWM*

Below left: Discovering the 'mysteries of the Orient' are two (armed) RASC soldiers, trying out a hubble-bubble pipe outside a giftshop in Kuwait. British troops were sent to Kuwait in July 1961, at the request of the ruler, to assist in defence against any possible attempts by Iraq to annex the sheikdom. *IWM*

Above right: A visit to the Tiger Balm Gardens was always a firm favourite during a sightseeing trip in Singapore. The gardens feature dozens of tableaux telling ancient legends of the Orient, as well as miniature replicas of Chinese buildings and temples.

Right: Buying carpets from an attractive assistant in a Cyprus gift shop.

Far right: Sightseeing in Georgetown, capital of British Guiana are these soldiers of 1 DERR, sent to the colony to restore and maintain law and order in February 1962. *IWM*

ALI THOMSON STORE

Above left: The giftshops of Steamer Point, Aden, were famous for their stocks of duty-free goods, which, after a little hard bargaining could be had at a remarkably low price.

Far left: Fancy a juicy water melon? There are plenty of them and many other tropical fruits on this stall in the free port of Aden.

Left: Sightseeing in Tripoli. Men of the Queen's Bays, stationed at Sabratha, had plenty of historic sites to visit such as Leptis Magna, May 1957. *IWM*

Above: RMPs on the Zone Border between East and West Germany, August 1961. *PR Berlin Bde*

Right: Manning a radio-relay post miles from anywhere in the Libyan desert are two Black Watch signallers. *PR Army*

Left: A young Military Police NCO raises the Union Jack at the Allied Kommandantura in Berlin. *PR Berlin Bde*

Below: A sapper of the Field Survey Detachment, RE, gives water to local women near Garissa in the northern frontier province of Kenya, March 1959. *PR Army*

Right: A fantastic place for an exercise! Right on the equator on the northern slopes of Mount Kenya, February 1961. *PR Army*

Far right: Trying on masks at a stall in Nairobi, whilst the pretty salesgirl watches, looking suitably winsome. *IWM*

Some National Servicemen had the good fortune to serve with units outside the British Army proper. One of these was Peter Jackson, who was commissioned from Mons OCS and posted (still 18) to serve with the Royal West African Field Force. He joined 2nd Light Battery WAA, who were then armed with the last remaining screw-guns, the 3.7in howitzers. It was a marvellously interesting and at times, taxing life. Peter told me many stories of his days with those 'warm, wild, wonderful people' as he put it. My favourite is about one of the first interviews he had as a troop officer, when one of his men asked if he could change his black skin for a white one at the QM stores! Peter, after some thought, told him to leave his black skin with him for a few days whilst he tried to get a white replacement. The soldier changed his mind!

Right: 'For you all love the screw guns — the screw guns they all love you!' *P. Jackson*

Parades

Probably the most frequent parade that required a lot more effort than normal morning inspections and one which every National Serviceman attended, was Guard Mounting. In some units an extra man was always detailed on orders, so that a 'stick man' could be chosen — ie the smartest man on parade. He was then excused guard, although his name still appeared in the book as having completed a duty. Some keen types went to great lengths to be chosen, being carried on to the square by their mates so as not get their boots dusty, or spoil their knife edge creases!

Above: 'Guard to the guardroom dismiss!' A very smart main gate guard at 64th Training Regiment, RA, Oswestry, gives an immaculate butt salute (denoting officer on parade) before falling out to the guardroom hut behind them. Well done lovely boys! *RA Institution*

Right: The Orderly Officer inspects a well turned out guard from the Prince of Wales's Own Regiment of Yorkshire, during its tour of duty in Gibraltar, 1960. *IWM*

Above left: 'Cut out that grinning lad, or I'll make you smile on the other side of your face!' practising fixing and unfixing bayonets appears to amuse some of this RAOC guard. *R. J. Hale*

Centre left: Of course bands make a difference to any parade. The skirl of the pipes, the fabulous cacophony of sound of a regimental brass band, does much to lift the heart of any soldier. The band of the PWO accompanies the regimental guard during a guard mounting ceremony in Gibraltar, June 1960. *IWM*

Below: The pipers of the KOSB put in some practice at Batu Bahat Barracks, Malaya, December 1957. *IWM*

MP

52
21 Z S 65

Here are just a few of the photographs of parades sent to me from all over the world

Top far left: A big parade in familiar surroundings. Men of Aldershot Garrison — 'Home of the British Army' — march past the saluting base during the Centenary celebrations, 21 April 1954. *Soldier*

Top left: Even MPs get inspected sometimes! Military Policemen of the 11th Armoured Divison on parade for the GOC's inspection, Herford BAOR, 1955. *M. J. Booker*

Centre left: The CO of 22 LAA Regt, RA, waits at the saluting base in Menden, West Germany, to take the salute of his regiment on the King's Birthday Parade, 1949. *T. Coleman*

Bottom left: Centurions dip their guns in salute during the march past at Münster, West Germany, during the Coronation Parade 1953. *G. Forty*

Top right: The Governor salutes the colours during this spectacular parade held in Aden, 1961.

Above centre right: The poppies behind the capbadges are a sure sign that this was a Remembrance Day parade in Malaya, November 1954. *R. J. Hale*

Below centre right: HM The Queen's Birthday Parade, Johore Bahru, 10 June 1954. *Lt-Col A. J. Barker*

Bottom right: In 1949, the entire armoured might of 7th Armoured Division held a mounted parade for the Minister of War ('Manny' Shinwell) at the 'Windmill' on the Sennelager Training Area in West Germany. *G. Forty*

Sports and sportsmen

Another part of Service life which was enjoyed by nearly every National Serviceman was sport. Of course the facilities varied from place to place, but as the photos show, one could still have fun even if the pitch didn't quite match up to Wembley Stadium.

Right: Relaxing after jungle operations with a game of badminton in their isolated camp on a rubber estate in North Johore, are these soldiers of the Cameronians. Note the 'short' shorts!

Below right: A game of basketball in progress at Yong Peng camp, Malaya, December 1957. *IWM*

Above left: Basketball on roller skates is even more difficult! *Soldier*

Centre left: A welter weight bout in progress in the FARELF team boxing finals.

Below: A knock about game of football in progress at Yong Peng, Malaya, December 1957. *IWM*

Top left: Sappers and men of the PWO play hockey in Gibraltar, June 1960. *IWM*

Left: The 'Invincible' Dukes do it again! L Cpl Norman Field, who later played rugby league for Batley and Great Britain, scores a try for the battalion against an Ulster XV, 30 September 1959. The Dukes beat the Ulster XV by 19 points to 5. *J. Scroby*

Top: Gunners from 43 LAA Regiment, RA, get ski instruction from one of their officers at the Services Winter Leave Centre in the Troodos Mountains, Cyprus. *IWM*

Above: There were some magnificent swimming pools all over the Far East, like this one at Kuala Lumpur, being used by men of 55 Company, RASC, November 1957. *IWM*

Right: This is the life! Two members of the Aden Services Yachting Club sail one of the boats donated by the Nuffield Trust, during a race, 1961.

Right: 'Take it back there!'
1 Squadron, Royal Signals Tug of War Team in the Canal Zone, September 1954. *J. Mann*

Below: The Guards water polo team in action under the palms of Aden, 1961.

National Service brought a great wealth of sporting talent into the Services. The Director of the Army Sports Control Board sent me the names of some 49 footballers, 24 rugby players, 13 cricketers and 12 hockey players, all of whom represented their country at international level whilst doing their National Service in the Army. And of course there were many others in all sports, including those who gained the ultimate accolade for sportsman and took part in the Olympic Games. Unfortunately there isn't room to put in all their photographs, but the small selection below may give some idea of the talent available. Of course this did lead sometimes to deliberate 'packing' of teams — particularly by training regiments, who naturally had first pick of the recruits when they joined. How many NS sportsmen were kept willingly or unwillingly on the staff of a training regiment in UK, so that they could play sport for them?

Left: Cpl Jack Scroby of 1 DWR shakes hands with the President of the Northern Ireland RUFC before a game between the regiment and an Ulster XV. Jack played rugby league for Halifax and Huddersfield after his demob and now devotes his spare time to coaching youngsters. The Dukes team that year (1959) contained a number of other famous players including NS men Derek Davies (Bradford Northern), Norman Field (Featherstone Rovers) and Paul Davies (Blackheath). *J. Scroby*

Centre far left: Doug Padgett, the Yorkshire and England cricketer spent his National Service as a PTI at 7 Training Regiment, Royal Signals, Catterick. He represented both the Army and the Combined Services and had: 'many happy times . . . and has never regretted the experience.' *D. Padgett*

Centre left: No 7 Training Regiment, Royal Signals Cricket XI, 1953. In addition to Doug Padgett (Yorks & England) 2nd from left back row, are other NS men viz: Gordon Barker (on his left) who opened for Essex for 20 years; Jim Wood (front row extreme left) of Lancs; F.G. Foulds (on his right) of Leics; Brian Frear (on Padgett's right) who was a professional footballer for many years with Huddersfield Town, Chesterfield and Halifax Town. *D. Padgett*

Bottom far left: Pte John Edrich of 20 Company, RASC, at the wheel of his army lorry. John played for the Army, Surrey and England. He is the cousin of brothers Bill (Middlesex), Geoffery (Lancashire), Brian (Glamorgan) and Eric (formerly of Lancashire). *Soldier*

Bottom left: Ready for action: Pte John Edrich had a great family reputation to maintain. He is wearing his Surrey second eleven badge. *Soldier*

Above: Not a National Serviceman to tangle with! 2391988 L Cpl Charnley, D. served with 9 Training Regiment, RE, as an assistant physical training instructor, but is better known as Dave Charnely, lightweight champion of Great Britain. *Soldier*

Above right: 'The Dartford Destroyer' Dave Charnley (wearing a headguard) spars with the Army light welter weight champion Gunner Dave Higgins, at Woolwich Barracks. *Soldier*

Right: There are some familiar faces among this group photo of the Army Football team at Woolwich, 30 October 1956, can you spot any of them? (Handling the cue is Duncan Edwards and to his left Bobby Charlton, just two of a star studded team which contained six internationals.) *Soldier*

Below: A very young Pte R. Charlton, RASC. At that time (1956), he was Manchester United's inside left and, as a contemporary sports report explained: '. . . is a player with a big future'. *Soldier*

Below right: L Cpl Duncan Edwards, RAOC, already had 10 full international caps and was an established star of Manchester United when this photo was taken. *Soldier*

Adventure training

Not strictly sport, not really military training, more like a mixture of the two. That is probably a fairly apt description of the Army Adventure Training scheme, which came in towards the end of the 1950s. Soldiers were encouraged to take part in tough, strenuous and character building exercises, either under supervision, or, as some of the photos show, completely 'doing their own thing', and getting a tremendous kick out of it. Of course many NS men were able to take part in this training and to do all sorts of things they would have never attempted in Civvy Street.

Left: Some regiments like the Duke of Wellington's ran their own adventure training schools. This one was the 'brain-child' of Scottish rugger international Capt David Gilbert-Smith MC, who started it in 1958, not long after the battalion had moved into Holywood Barracks, Belfast. It was set up in a wooded plateau overlooking Lough Larne and soldiers spent three weeeks there learning and practising tough outdoor activities which ended with a gruelling six day exercise. As part of an initiative test students improvised a raft to float a box of 'valuable instruments' across the 'shark infested' waters of the lough. *Soldier*

Below left: This section of the test demands ingenuity and sure footedness in traversing the tree stumps with the help of a piece of iron pipe. One slip and you were straight into the 'alligator swamp' below. *Soldier*

Below: Tree walks, jumping pits, etc were all to build up confidence for the 'big moment' — plunging 50ft down the 'Death Slide' into the cold and muddy lough. *Soldier*

Left: After some preliminary training on a quarry face near the camp, students tackled rock-climbing in the Mourne Mountains. *Soldier*

Below left: Triumphant end to the course's big exercise. In their role as terrorists, two canoeists 'sink' a cross-Channel ferry at Larne Quay, by chalking their unit name on her water-line. *Soldier*

Below: Back in barracks, members of the Adventure Club, spend their evenings building canoes for more adventure training. *Soldier*

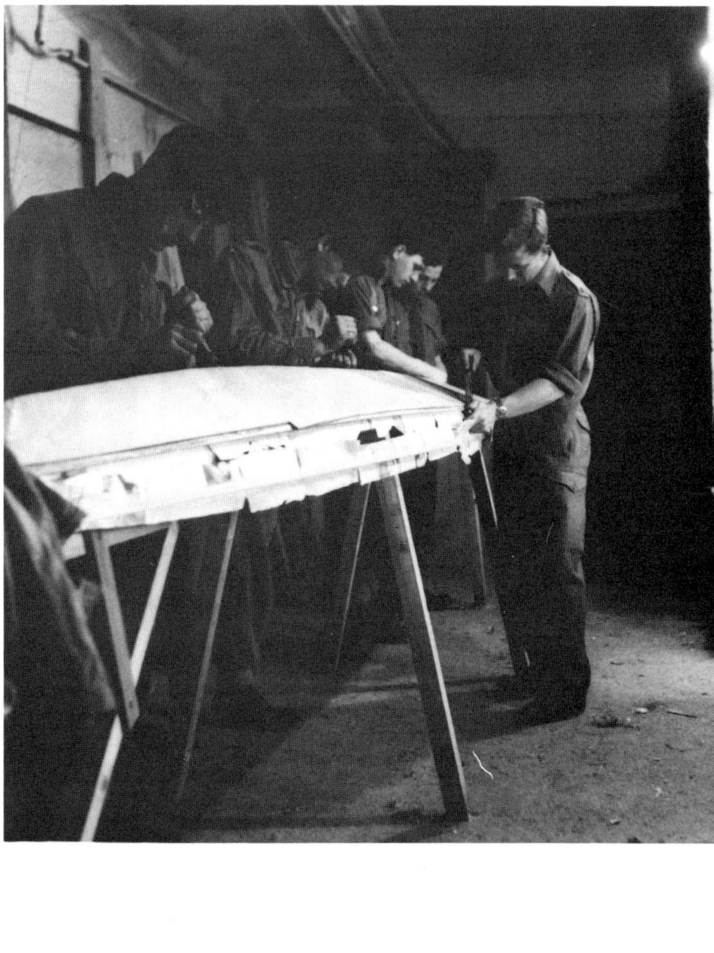

Top: Further afield, men of 1 Staffs have an early morning dip in a pool near their camp on the northern slope of Mount Kenya during an adventure training exercise. *PR Army*

Bill Ashby was one of a very lucky party who went off from Singapore on an adventure training expedition to an offshore tropical island. He writes: '. . . a few of us, armed with the necessary equipment of army "compo" rations and hay-boxes (full of beer), chartered a local fishing boat to drop us on an island off the east coast of Malaya. It was surrounded by coral which barred our way at first. We landed and made camp on the beach not knowing whether it was inhabited. A couple of days later we found a small fishing village and made friends with the locals. They challenged us to a football match which we were honour-bound to accept. The pitch had coconut trees all over it which the ball rebounded off, but were useful at half time when one of our rival team climbed up to get a supply of fresh coconut milk. We spent a week "stranded" on our tropic isle until our prearranged rescue by the fishing boat.'

Right: Boarding the fishing boat, note the hay-boxes full of beer. *W. Ashby*

Above: Camp on the tropical island — Robinson Crusoe never had it so good! *W. Ashby*

The dear old NAAFI

Servitor Servientum (the servant of those who serve)

The haven of comfort in most camps, especially the more out of the way ones, was the NAAFI (Navy, Army and Air Forces Institute), whose breaktime tea and buns helped many to manage not to expire from starvation during a strenuous morning's training. Some spent all their pay in the *Naffy*, as it was normally called, on cigarettes, sweets, cups of tea and cakes, beans and chips or similar hot meals — others of course drank it all away in the beer bar. Money, or the lack of it, was always a problem, nobody having any at the beginning of the week, except for the naturally thrifty. Being a non-smoker helped of course, but most were still spent up by Sunday evening. For its part the NAAFI after World War II had to carry out a severe slimming down process, but still try to maintain its worldwide service. Until the end of National Service there were still plenty of customers and large amounts were spent on building modern, well appointed clubs in towns around the UK. The programme was for 12 clubs to be built by the mid-fifties. Portsmouth was the first to be opened in January 1946, and thereafter other clubs followed at less than yearly intervals in Colchester, Chatham, Aldershot, Oswestry, Catterick, Bicester, Plymouth, Lincoln, Chippenham, Glasgow and Salisbury. As the photos show, they contained restaurants, lounges, bars and taverns, reading and writing rooms, music and TV rooms, games and ballrooms, and at some, residential facilities. There were also town clubs abroad, such as the one in Singapore (the *Britannia*) opened in 1952. And of course NAAFI was doing all it could to modernise its image. A new and smarter uniform for the NAAFI girls was introduced, so that they looked less like 'Little Orphan Annie', but could the new look have had anything to do with the high marriage rate — one newspaper calculated that they got married at the rate of one every 37 hours! Canteens too were slowly changed as Harry Miller explained in his excellent book, *Service to the Services*: '. . . the old image of beer slopped on the floor and initials carved in the table top was fading; indeed milk was fast becoming a more popular drink than beer . . . Noise was part of the amenity and juke boxes were installed in many canteens . . . Vending machines, which had been used on a small scale during the war, began to spread . . . but it has taken a long time to get the customer reconciled to the absence of a NAAFI girl: you cannot swop banter with a machine.'

Right: Even in 1956 NAAFI was still spread across 40 different countries. Typical of the many unit canteens all over the world is this breaktime scene 'somewhere in England'.
Miss Daniell's Soldiers' Home

Above: Mobile canteens, like these which catered for a Coronation parade in BAOR in 1953, were widely used by NAAFI. For example, during the autumn manoeuvres in 1954, NAAFI ran 33 mobiles for the 137,000 troops taking part. *HQ NAAFI*

Left: Korean veterans will recognise the thatched NAAFI roadhouse in Korea, 1953. *G. Forty*

Below left: Cafeteria in the Chatham Club, one of the 12 'town clubs' opened in the UK to cater for all three Services. *HQ NAAFI*

Above: The Tavern Bar of the Glasgow town club rivalled most locals. *HQ NAAFI*

Right: Juke boxes were introduced into clubs in the 1950s, like this one in the Aldershot Club. *HQ NAAFI*

Below right: Abroad, NAAFI Clubs were just as good, if not better, with facilities to rival the most expensive private clubs. NAAFI kiosk at the 'Old Victorian' Lido, Fayid, Canal Zone. *HQ NAAFI*

Above left: Yes this is a NAAFI! The Other Ranks 'Old Victorian' Lido at Fayid. *HQ NAAFI*

Centre left: The Mermaid Club, Steamer Point Aden. This club served the whole garrison and was located next to the main headquarters. It had marvellous facilities including safe bathing (protected by shark proof nets), a sea water swimming pool, excellent hockey and football pitches, floodlit tennis courts, plus all the usual NAAFI club facilities. *HQ NAAFI*

As well as the clubs, NAAFI operated leave centres all over the world for all ranks and their families. Perhaps these photos will bring back happy memories of holidays spent learning to ski in Germany, or basking on the beach in Egypt and Kenya. Undoubtedly they were a marvellous experience for those lucky enough to be able to visit them. They were of course heavily subsidised, so that their rates were within the reach of all pockets.

Below left: New arrivals are welcomed by one of the German stewards at the Winterberg Leave Centre. *HQ NAAFI*

Below: The dining room of the Sea View Holiday Camp, Port Fouad, Egypt. *HQ NAAFI*

Above right: Chatting up the staff in the Services Shop at the Sea View Holiday Camp. His line of chat clearly has 'turned the head' of the girl on the left! *HQ NAAFI*

Centre right: Silversands Leave Centre, near Mombasa on the East African coast, had to be given up when British troops pulled out of Aden. Guests lived in 'bandas' (bungalows) and there was a well stocked bar, library, film shows, dances, stage shows, trips and safaris. *HQ NAAFI*

But even the NAAFI had its share of bumf!

Below: Remember this NAAFI Ration chit? *Adam Forty*

Below right: Travel voucher for the leave centre on the Mohne See. *Adam Forty*

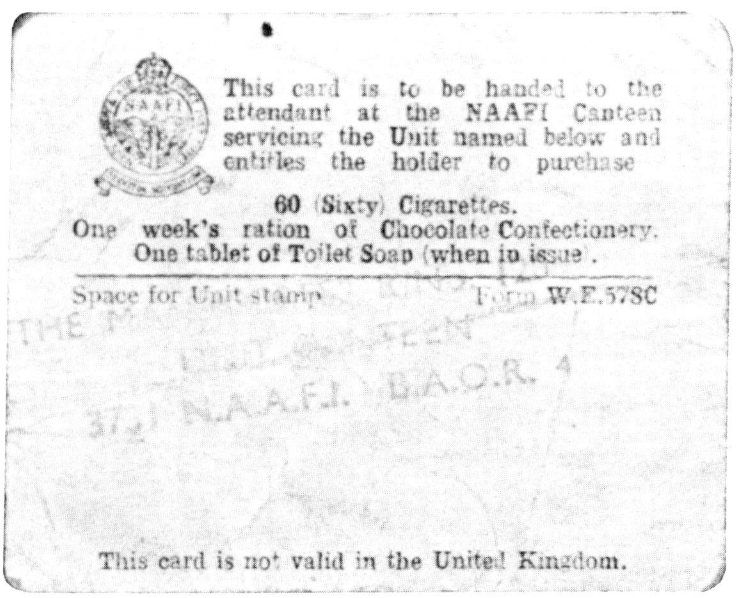

This card is to be handed to the attendant at the NAAFI Canteen servicing the Unit named below and entitles the holder to purchase

60 (Sixty) Cigarettes.
One week's ration of Chocolate Confectionery.
One tablet of Toilet Soap (when in issue).

Space for Unit stamp — Form W.E.578C

N.A.A.F.I. B.A.O.R. 4

This card is not valid in the United Kingdom.

SERIAL No 2277 PRICE - ADULT 2/6
CHILD (3-14y) 1/3

No 3 LEAVE CENTRE, MOHNE SEE.

ENTITLES HOLDER TO TRAVEL FROM DETRAINING STATION - HOTEL - ENTRAINING STATION.

NB - CHILDREN UNDER 3 YEARS TRAVEL FREE.

THIS CHARGE IS LEVIED IN ACCORDANCE WITH BAOR GRO 7228/1951.

Other havens

Of course NAAFI was not the only organisation that looked after comforts for the troops. There were also the wonderful voluntary organisations such as Toc H, the YMCA, Church Army, Church of Scotland, the WRVS, and the Soldiers' Homes, namely Miss Daniell's in Aldershot and the more widespread Sandes Homes. Also of course, whilst soldiers were in hospital, then the British Red Cross and St John's Ambulance did their share. This short chapter is a tribute to all these fabulous organisations who have done (and are continuing to do) so much to help British soldiers everywhere. The photos show but a few of their many activities.

Above: The cup that cheers. Could there be a better advertisement for Toc H than this soldier's cheerful grin? *Toc H*

Right: A typical Toc H Services club in BAOR (this one is in Berlin), where privately rented houses near the barracks provided a haven of peace. Toc H of course began in just such a privately rented house in the small town of Poperinge in the Ypres salient in Belgium in 1915. It was called 'Talbot House', hence the now familiar name 'Toc H', which was World War 1 telegraphese for the initials TH. Seven miles only behind the front line, 'Everyman's Club', as it was called, provided comfort and companionship to the grandfathers of many NS men. *Toc H*

Above: Morning break in a YMCA canteen in Osnabruck, Germany. The YMCA began even earlier than Toc H, the first recorded incident of YMCA volunteers operating with Servicemen being during the American Civil War, when they served *both* sides on the battlefields with an ad hoc mobile canteen. Such establishments as their Tottenham Court Road YMCA club in London, will long be remembered by thousands of grateful Servicemen. *YMCA*

Centre right: Even out on the training areas the WRVS (WVS until 1966) did their stuff. WVS Service Welfare Members worked in most units, usually under the sponsorship of the NAAFI. They will be remembered with affection for their motherly approach in dealing with soldiers' problems. *WRVS*

Below right: This super swimming pool was a feature of the Sandes Soldiers' Home in Singapore. *W. Ashby*

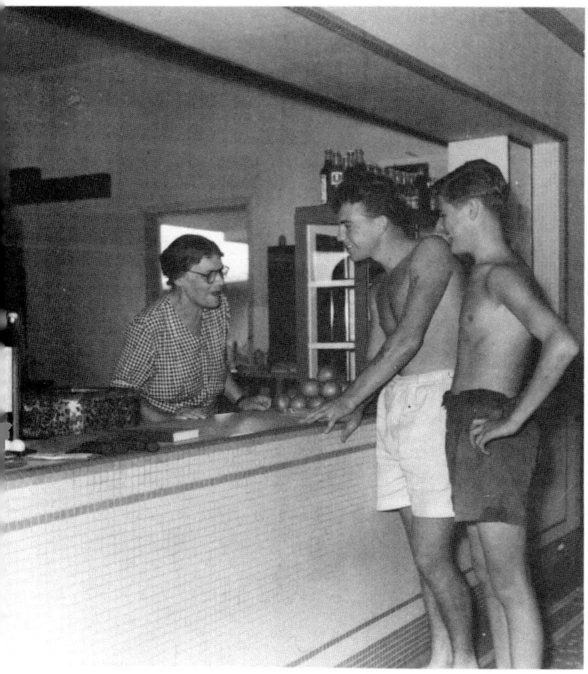

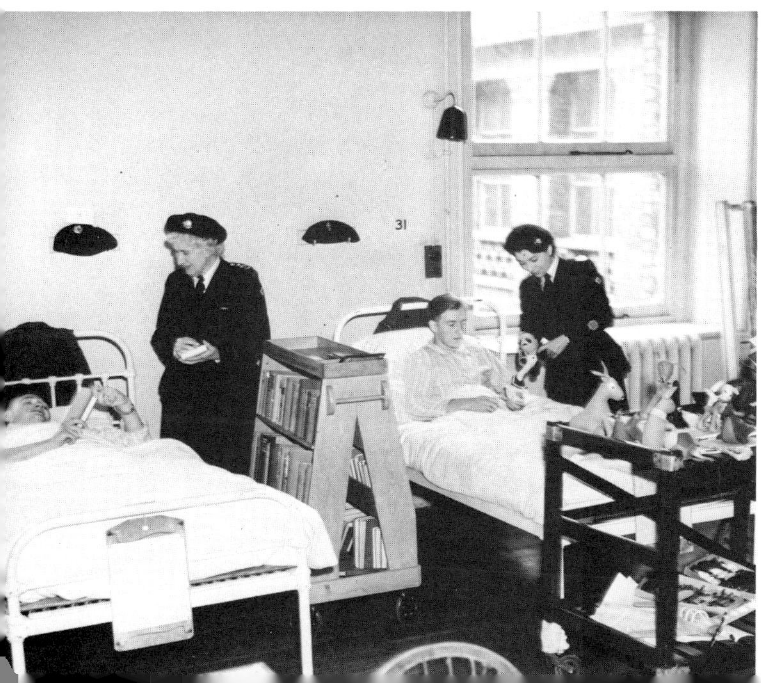

Top left: Those who stayed at the Sandes Home in Singapore will remember with affection Miss Leslie Symes, pictured here in January 1956. *Soldier*

Top: Sandes Home at Catterick, probably the most well remembered building in the garrison. How many million cuppas did they dole out? *Sandes Soldiers' Homes*

Above left: Miss Daniell's Soldiers' Home Aldershot was a firm favourite with the whole garrison. *Miss Daniell's Soldiers Home*

Above: The Daniell's tent at the Aldershot Horse Show was always very popular. *Miss Daniell's Soldiers Home*

Left: British Red Cross workers provide men in hospital with books to read and hobbies to pursue. *British Red Cross Society*

The doors that never closed

Home from home for Servicemen on leave or passing through London, was the old Union Jack Club near Waterloo (now rebuilt). Every Serviceman below commissioned rank was automatically a member of this famous club, which was opened by HM King Edward VII in 1907. In its first 50 years it had catered for nearly nine million guests, including soldiers from many other countries. The five storey red-brick building which was just a stone's throw away from Waterloo station, was enlarged four times, the last occasion being when Lord Nuffield gave £30,000 for an annexe to be built in 1940. In 1957, a night's lodging (including breakfast) cost 6 shillings and 6 pence ($32\frac{1}{2}$ new pence!) Soldiers stationed in UK could stay for 14 days at a stretch and those from abroad for 28 days. The club was non profitmaking as is the new UJ Club, and was run by a council representing all three Services, and a general committee composed of other ranks elected by the representative members of 175 major Service units in Britain. Those who stayed there will remember the Memorial Corridor with its complete roll of all holders of the Victoria Cross.

Above: The front steps of the Union Jack Club. Like the 'Windmill' Theatre it 'never closed'. *Soldier*

Below: Any rooms? Booking in at the reception desk. *Soldier*

Right: One of the spacious public rooms. *Soldier*

Left: Passers-by hunted in vain for the Union Jack Club's shop — it was indoors, down in the basement. *Soldier*

Below left and below: The Union Jack Club had good facilities where men could do their own washing and ironing. *Soldier*

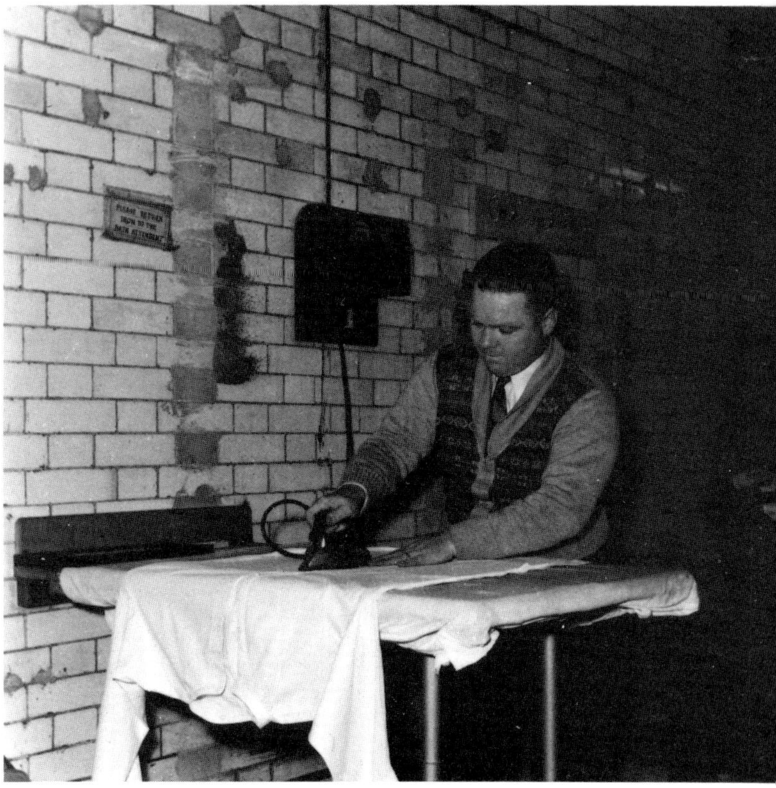

Right: Probably millions have used this cigarette lighter which had been burning ever since World War 1. *Soldier*

Below: No excuse for missing the last train to barracks — a familiar noticeboard in the club. *Soldier*

Entertainment

As well as the NAAFI and the voluntary bodies who ran clubs, there were many other people who helped to entertain the troops, especially whilst they were serving abroad. Organisations such as the Forces Broadcasting Service (now the BFBS), and the Army Kinema Corporation (now the SKC) ran radio stations and cinemas all over the world. In addition, many famous entertainers, such as Harry Secombe, Peter Sellers, Russ Conway, Anne Shelton, Ted Ray, and many, many others, gave up their time to go out with CSEU concert parties and shows for the troops. And don't let us forget here the ever helpful WVS 'Mums' in units, who did their bit to make each and every soldier's life not quite as 'terrible ard' as it might have been. Everyone who has been in uniform has much to thank them for.

Left: The AKC, now amalgamated since 1969 with the RAF Cinema Corporation to form the Services Kinema Corporation (SKC), ran cinemas all over the world like this one at Selerang Camp, Singapore. *IWM*

Right: The opening of the new Globe Cinema at Barton Stacey camp was celebrated by the personal appearance of the star of the film, Miss Jill Adams. *SKC*

Centre right: Barbara Kelly and the late Gilbert Harding are seen here making for the stage of the Globe Cinema, Aborfield, to take part in a 'live' show — probably a radio panel game or chat show. *SKC*

Bottom right: The British Forces Broadcasting Services (BFBS) does marvellous work entertaining troops all over the world. Those who served in BAOR will remember, for example, the British Forces Network (BFN). Here, Miss Barbara Garner makes an announcement at a BFBS radio station in Gibraltar. *BFBS*

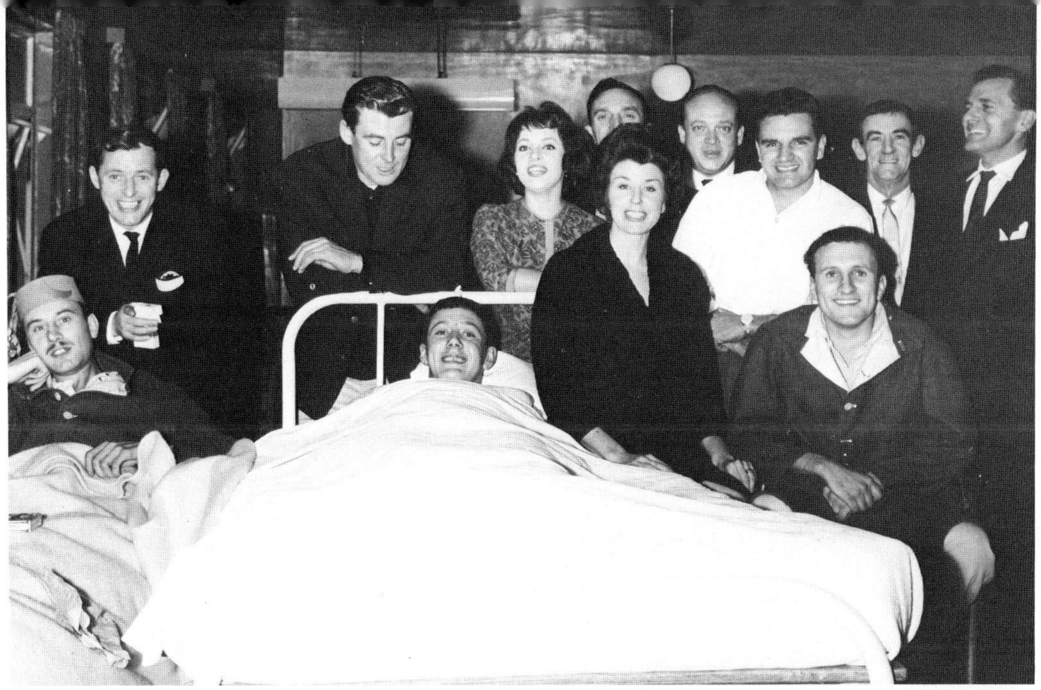

Above left: Russ Conway and other members of the CSEU show, visit troops in Dhekelia Hospital, Cyprus, 1961. *CSEU*

Above: Bookshops, like this one run by the YMCA in Berlin, provided books, magazines (and comics!) for the troops. *YMCA*

Left: A Church Service after tea on Sundays was a feature of Miss Daniell's Soldier's Home at Aldershot.
Miss Daniell's Soldier's Home

Below left: Of course some times the soldiers themselves provided the entertainment, like this successful band. *Soldier*

Boozing

Most soldiers like to drink and National Servicemen in khaki were no exception, as the accompanying photos show. NS pay went further abroad in duty-free stations such as the British Army of the Rhine — called by some 'The British Army of the Wine' for obvious reasons! Despite this however, the British soldier of the National Service era was probably the most abstemious in history. Indeed in 1961 for every 10 glasses of beer sold by NAAFI nine glasses of milk, 50 cups of tea, 15 soft drinks and 10 cups of coffee were consumed. A sobering thought!

Right: Bad Man's Gulch. Relaxing in their jungle canteen are these men of the Cameronians, after returning from anti-bandit operations.

Below right: The inscription on the back of this photo reads: 'Officers' Mess, Menden, Germany at 3am — it's a good job that neither the Provost Sgt nor the Mess Sgt were around at the time!
T. Coleman

Above left: Time to relax at a Christmas party in the Malayan jungle, 1949. *A. D. Barrowcliff*

Centre left: Ron Wingham and friend clearly like Cyprus beer. *R. Wingham*

Below left and below: Michael Booker sent me these photos of himself and friends letting their hair down — they don't appear to be doing too badly, despite the fact that they were all Military Policemen! *M. Booker*

Above: Very easy in the cold light of day, but I doubt if anyone else featured in the other photos in this chapter could have passed the test (RSM Brittain excepted of course!) This photo was taken at a regimental sports day held by 64th Training Regiment RA, at Oswestry, 26 March 1956.
RA Institution

Right: Lubrication for the loudest voice in the British Army. RSM Brittain downs a cooling draught of ale after receiving his Long Service and Good Conduct Medal.
Soldier

Demob

All good (and bad) things have to come to an end, and eventually the days left to cross off on the 'Days to Do Chuff Chart' or whatever the calendar kept by most NS men was called, were whittled down to the brief few that would allow for the process of demobilisation. Of course if one were serving in the Far East in the early days, when travel was by trooper, then the last few days were extended by at least a month of travelling time. The Army's farewell to its National Servicemen was a very personal affair with units choosing their own special way of saying goodbye. Some held parades, others made presentations, the RAOC Depot at Blackdown presented their last NS recruit with a clock; the RASC gave their's an inscribed plaque; the last three conscripts to serve with 38 Corps Engineer Regiment were presented with inscribed tankards, whilst the last gunner on the staff of the School of Artillery at Manorbier, received a silver cigarette case from his regular comrades, presented by his battery commander at an all-ranks dance. At Shorncliffe, the 1st Battalion, The Royal Sussex Regiment, paraded with band, drums and colours in a stirring tribute to their last 20 National Servicemen, whilst the Duke of Wellington's Regiment honoured 94 departing conscripts with a similar parade, as the photos below show. Kit was handed in, the inevitable mass of documents and forms signed and issued (I have included a selection), then at long last they were free! — well almost free, because there was still the little matter of attending for their part-time service with the Territorial Army — but that's another story!

Left: Going home, with suitably stencilled kitbags. *A. Ward*

Above right: Heavily laden but cheerfully willing to carry twice as much, are these men of the Cameronians embarking in the *Empire Halladale* after the battalion had spent three years of operations against the Communist terrorists in Malaya.

Centre right: 'Goodbye Malaya'. Men of the Royal Dragoons on board the troopship *Oxfordshire* before she left Singapore.

Below: Handcuffed and well escorted L Cpl McGee, last RMP National Serviceman is dragged to Dusseldorf airport from Caernarvon Barracks.
Sgt A. R. Bleese

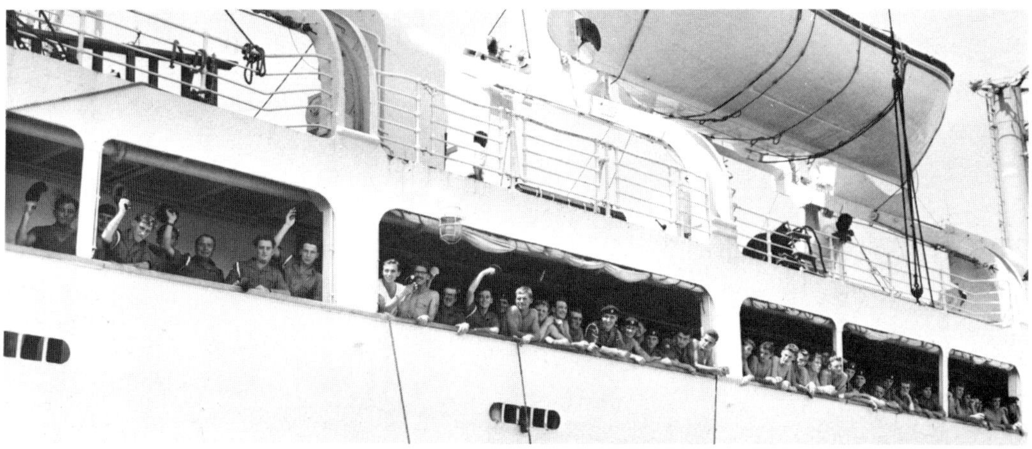

Top: With a handshake and a word of thanks, Lt Col A.B.M. Kavanagh MC, says a personal farewell to his National Service 'Dukes'. *Soldier*

Above: The last detail was handing in one's kit. *Soldier*

Right: These boots will probably not do any more marching. *Soldier*

Above: 'How much did he say we had to pay for a missing housewife?' *Soldier*

Above right: Sometimes the excitement of it all was just a bit too much. *Soldier*

Below left: Kitbags with no troubles to pack up in them — I'm free! *Soldier*

Right: Or am I? National Service reservists on their 15 days annual TA camp, look quite resigned to being 'back in the old routine' with 7th Warwicks TA. *P. J. Rafferty*

Below: 'The purpose of this pamphlet is to help you in the change over from Service to Civilian life. It contains information on a number of Service and other matters which will be of importance to you in the period immediately following completion of your Active Army service . . .' (Extract from Introduction). *Adam Forty*

Below right: Book issued to those NS men who were needed for immediate recall in the event of a National Emergency. *Adam Forty*

FOR YOUR GUIDANCE

READ THIS AND KEEP IT CAREFULLY

WHAT TO DO ON LEAVING THE ACTIVE ARMY, AND HOW TO DO IT

For issue to National Service Officers and Men called up under the National Service Acts 1948, and to Regular Soldiers and members of the Women's Services who leave the Active Army

(Revised January, 1955)

ISSUED BY THE WAR OFFICE AND THE MINISTRY OF LABOUR AND NATIONAL SERVICE

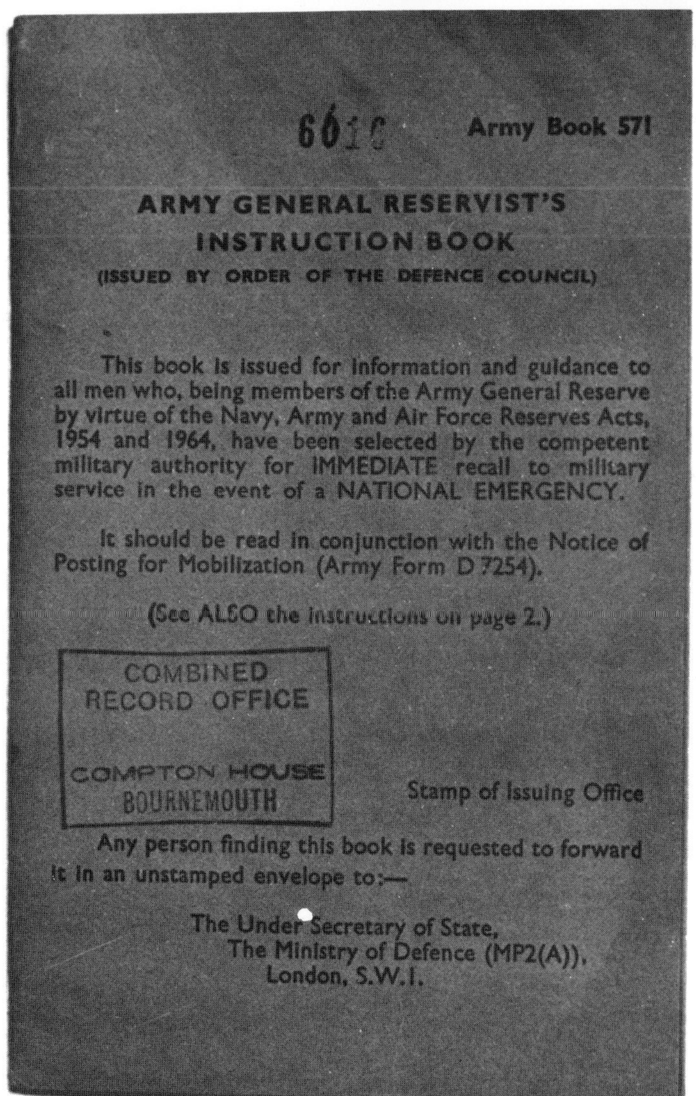

Army Book 571

ARMY GENERAL RESERVIST'S INSTRUCTION BOOK

(ISSUED BY ORDER OF THE DEFENCE COUNCIL)

This book is issued for information and guidance to all men who, being members of the Army General Reserve by virtue of the Navy, Army and Air Force Reserves Acts, 1954 and 1964, have been selected by the competent military authority for IMMEDIATE recall to military service in the event of a NATIONAL EMERGENCY.

It should be read in conjunction with the Notice of Posting for Mobilization (Army Form D 7254).

(See ALSO the instructions on page 2.)

COMBINED RECORD OFFICE COMPTON HOUSE BOURNEMOUTH

Stamp of Issuing Office

Any person finding this book is requested to forward it in an unstamped envelope to:—

The Under Secretary of State,
The Ministry of Defence (MP2(A)),
London, S.W.1.

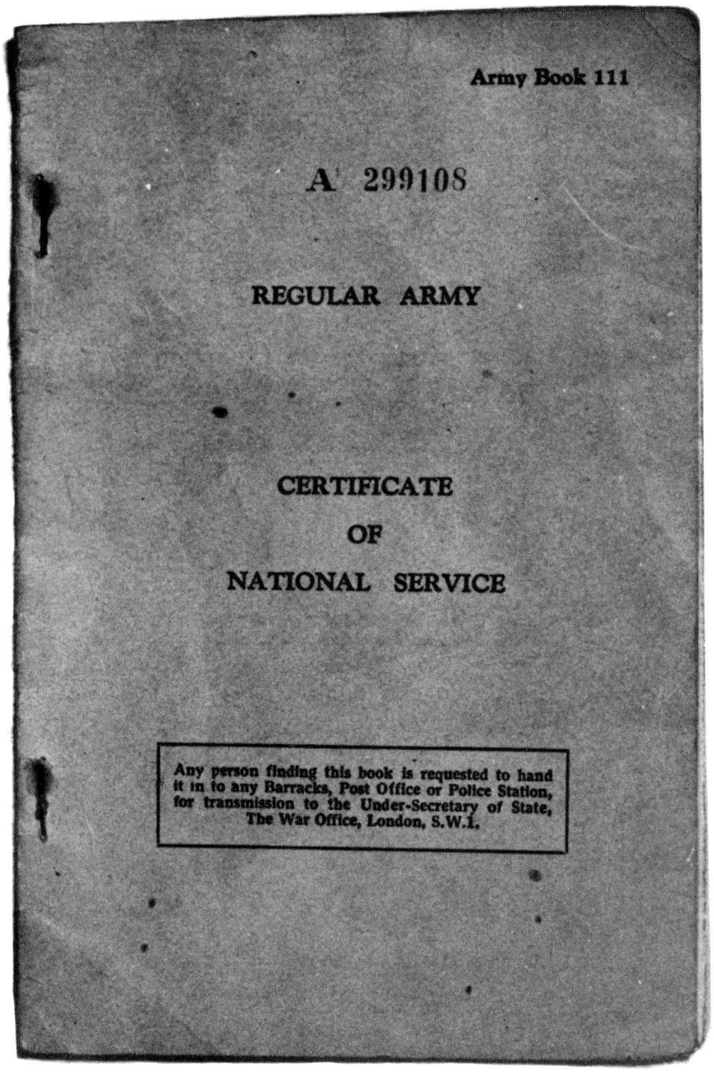

Army Book 111

A 299108

REGULAR ARMY

CERTIFICATE OF NATIONAL SERVICE

Any person finding this book is requested to hand it in to any Barracks, Post Office or Police Station, for transmission to the Under-Secretary of State, The War Office, London, S.W.1.

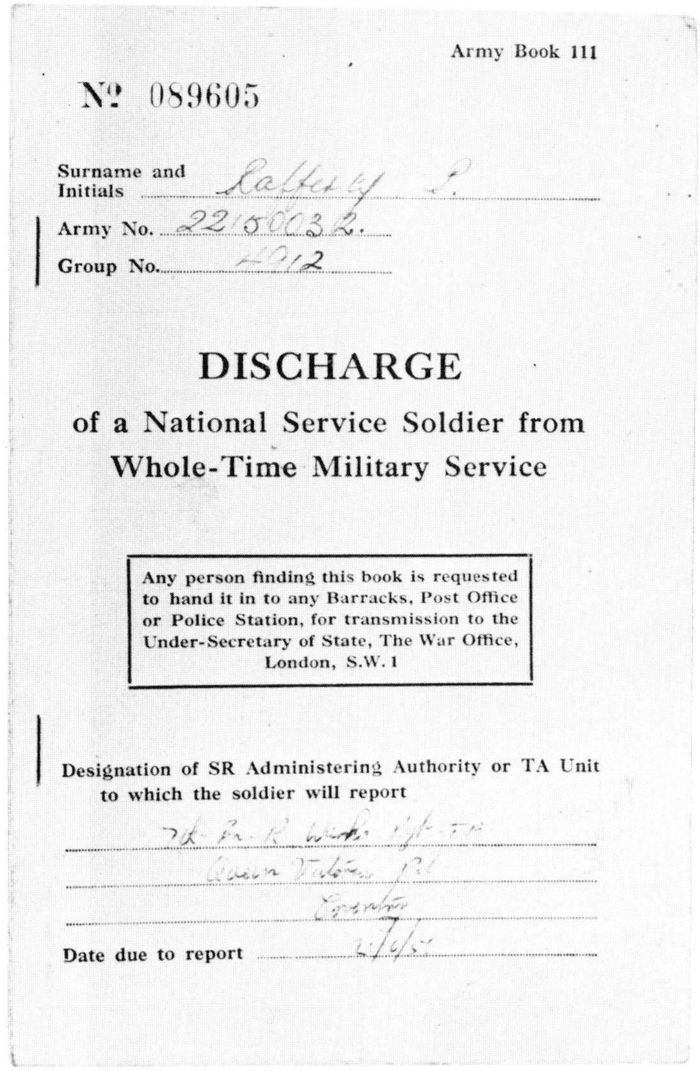

Army Book 111

№ 089605

Surname and Initials: Rafferty P.

Army No.: 22150032.

Group No.: 4012

DISCHARGE

of a National Service Soldier from Whole-Time Military Service

Any person finding this book is requested to hand it in to any Barracks, Post Office or Police Station, for transmission to the Under-Secretary of State, The War Office, London, S.W. 1

Designation of SR Administering Authority or TA Unit to which the soldier will report

Date due to report

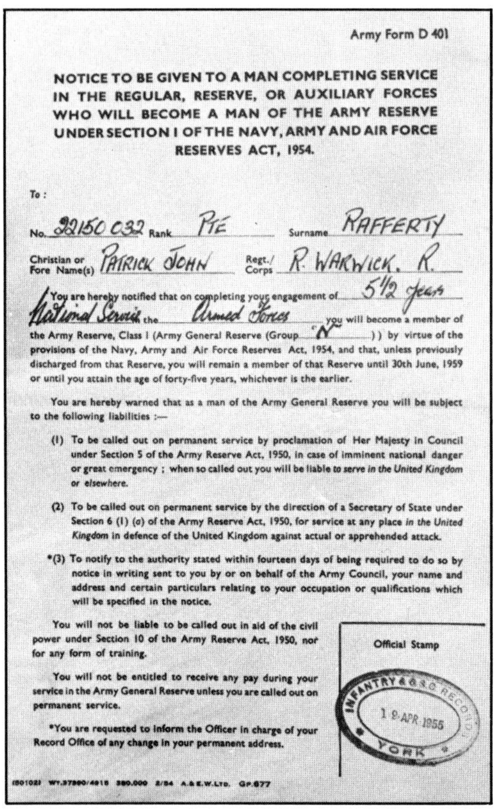

Army Form D 401

NOTICE TO BE GIVEN TO A MAN COMPLETING SERVICE IN THE REGULAR, RESERVE, OR AUXILIARY FORCES WHO WILL BECOME A MAN OF THE ARMY RESERVE UNDER SECTION I OF THE NAVY, ARMY AND AIR FORCE RESERVES ACT, 1954.

To:

No. 22150032 Rank PTE Surname RAFFERTY

Christian or Fore Name(s) PATRICK JOHN Regt./Corps R. WARWICK. R.

You are hereby notified that on completing your engagement of 5½ years National Service in the Armed Forces you will become a member of the Army Reserve, Class I (Army General Reserve (Group "N")) by virtue of the provisions of the Navy, Army and Air Force Reserves Act, 1954, and that, unless previously discharged from that Reserve, you will remain a member of that Reserve until 30th June, 1959 or until you attain the age of forty-five years, whichever is the earlier.

You are hereby warned that as a man of the Army General Reserve you will be subject to the following liabilities :—

(1) To be called out on permanent service by proclamation of Her Majesty in Council under Section 5 of the Army Reserve Act, 1950, in case of imminent national danger or great emergency ; when so called out you will be liable *to serve in the United Kingdom or elsewhere.*

(2) To be called out on permanent service by the direction of a Secretary of State under Section 6 (1) (*a*) of the Army Reserve Act, 1950, for service at any place *in the United Kingdom* in defence of the United Kingdom against actual or apprehended attack.

*(3) To notify to the authority stated within fourteen days of being required to do so by notice in writing sent to you by or on behalf of the Army Council, your name and address and certain particulars relating to your occupation or qualifications which will be specified in the notice.

You will not be liable to be called out in aid of the civil power under Section 10 of the Army Reserve Act, 1950, nor for any form of training.

You will not be entitled to receive any pay during your service in the Army General Reserve unless you are called out on permanent service.

*You are requested to inform the Officer in charge of your Record Office of any change in your permanent address.

Official Stamp

INFANTRY & G.S.C. RECORDS · 19 APR 1955 · YORK

(80102) WT.37990/4915 380,000 2/54 A.&E.W.LTD. GP.677

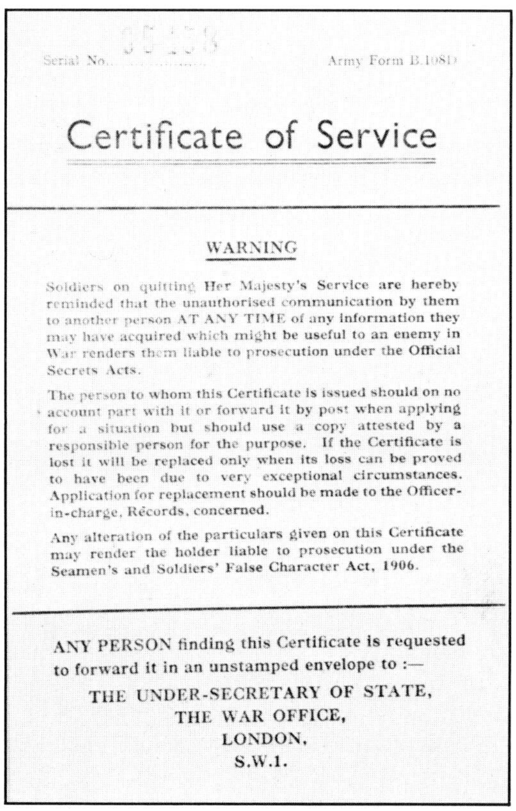

Serial No.

Army Form B.108D

Certificate of Service

WARNING

Soldiers on quitting Her Majesty's Service are hereby reminded that the unauthorised communication by them to another person AT ANY TIME of any information they may have acquired which might be useful to an enemy in War renders them liable to prosecution under the Official Secrets Acts.

The person to whom this Certificate is issued should on no account part with it or forward it by post when applying for a situation but should use a copy attested by a responsible person for the purpose. If the Certificate is lost it will be replaced only when its loss can be proved to have been due to very exceptional circumstances. Application for replacement should be made to the Officer-in-charge, Records, concerned.

Any alteration of the particulars given on this Certificate may render the holder liable to prosecution under the Seamen's and Soldiers' False Character Act, 1906.

ANY PERSON finding this Certificate is requested to forward it in an unstamped envelope to :—

THE UNDER-SECRETARY OF STATE,
THE WAR OFFICE,
LONDON,
S.W.1.

Above left: Certificate of National Service. This gave any would-be employer a brief picture of how you had got on in your service — it began with a Military Conduct grading which could be either: Very Good, Good, Fair, or Unsatisfactory depending upon the entries on your conduct sheets. *Adam Forty*

Above: Front cover of AB 111 discharge book — this was an older type of that shown in the last photo. *Adam Forty*

Far left: Notice regarding the Army General Reserve, AF D401. *Adam Forty*

Left: Certificate of Service issued after completion of *all* service, ie: this certificate was issued by the TA unit with whom the NS men had completed his part-time service. When you got one of these your really were free! *Adam Forty*

Mates

Many of those who wrote to me in the preparation of this book said that the thing they would remember most about their National Service was the comradeship. The 'mates' they made in those days were *the best*. They were all in the same boat, all had to put up with the same hardships, share the same jokes, the good moments and the bad — 'And those who then did stand by me, stand thus until eternity'. This last chapter is a tribute to all those mates wherever they now may be. Field Marshal Sir Gerald Templer said of the National Servicemen: 'Their gallantry was in the highest traditions of professional fighting men'; Earl Mountbatten said: 'Many lost their lives and we shall always remember them with great pride'. Certainly the Army will never be quite the same without them.

Above left: Mates from 9th Airborne Anti Tank Regiment, RA, Flensburg, 1949. *T. Coleman*

Below left: John Mann and friends pose beside a strange looking elephant fountain in Fayid. *J. Mann*

Top: A group of NS men of the Cameronians at Buxterhude, Germany, 1954. Dave Lynch who sent the photo was a cook in the battalion. He was so determined to make a good impression when he first arrived that he put lashings of extra sugar in the porridge at breakfast in the cookhouse — nobody at Aldershot had told him that the Scots ate it with salt! *D. Lynch*

Left: A RMP trio, plus mascot — sadly it was run over and killed shortly after this photo was taken. *M. Booker*

Above: Another group with a mascot, this time they were cooks of the ACC attached to the Royal Welch Fusiliers in BAOR. *E. J. Spurway*

Top right: Bill, Les, Royston, Peter, Brian, Russ and Keith in a Malayan sugar plantation, 1954. *R. J. Hale*

Top far right: Ready for guard mounting, 30 Battalion RAOC, Singapore 1955. *R. J. Hale*

Right: The best platoon in 'The Tigers', Malaya, October 1953. *A. D. Barrowcliff*

84
1st Q.O.R.W.K.
2 PLATOON "A" COMPANY
THE TIGERS
2 PLATOON

Top: Just back from a 'push up the jungle' to find terrorist food dumps. *A. Ward*

Above: Guardsmen on an exercise. *R. White*

Left: Derek and Des, June 1957. *D. Pilkington*

Right: A cheerful trio of radio operators belonging to the Signal Troop attached to 43 Field Regiment RA at Dortmund BAOR c1951/52. *W. Burnett*

RASC
MALTA
051697
B.J.